LIVING
FREE

LIVING
FREE

Lester Sumrall

A SCEPTRE BOOK
A DIVISION OF ROYAL PUBLISHERS

NASHVILLE

Library of Congress Cataloging in Publication Data

Sumrall, Lester Frank, 1913-
  Living free.

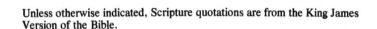

  Includes bibliographical references.
  1. Christian life—1960-   2. Mental health. I. Title.
BV4501.2.S845   248'.4   79-21233
ISBN 0-8407-5696-8

Contents

Introduction

Modern man has been led to believe that psychiatry has the answers to life's questions and dilemmas. According to *Time* magazine,

. . . psychiatry itself is now on the couch. . . . Psychiatrists themselves acknowledge that their profession often smacks of modern alchemy—full of jargon, obfuscation and mystification but precious little real knowledge. . . . Any diagnostic process that lends itself so readily to massive errors of this sort [an experiment in a psychiatric ward that backfired] cannot be a very reliable one. . . . Some critics predict that classical psychoanalysis will soon be extinct.[1]

What is modern man to do if his source of knowing how to cope with life is no longer considered reliable? With the rug of psychiatry pulled out from under his feet, where is modern man to turn? Is there any way he can live free from guilt, depression, and stress? How can he cope?

The development staff of Science Research Associates believes the answer to coping is within man himself.

You do have the capacity to learn how to cope with problems. . . . Coping also requires the ability to be realistic—to see things as they are, not as you think they should be. . . . When you know what the options are when a problem exists—or if you know where to find or create the options—then you know how to cope. . . . In taking greater responsibility for your life, you need to be able to distinguish between things that can be changed and things that cannot be changed. You can change a lot about yourself. . . . You also can change some of the conditions in the world about you. . . . Now coping is up to you.[2]

Do you have the resources within you to meet life head on?

As a minister of the gospel for fifty years, I can say with confidence that only if man is inhabited by Jesus Christ in the person of the Holy Spirit can he cope with life adequately. Christ is the resource within us that enables us to cope.

The material in this book has to do with the inner man, the spiritual man. It is my belief that man is composed of three parts: body, soul, and spirit.

When Adam sinned, he died. His spirit died, although his body lived on for another nine hundred and thirty years. For God had warned that if His commandment regarding the tree of good and evil were broken, "thou shalt surely die" (Gen. 2:17).

Through his spirit, Adam had experienced his relationship to God. His spirit was that which gave force and vitality to life; it died when Adam sinned.

When we place our faith in Christ, we are "reborn." Our spirit is "born again"; we are made "new creatures," and we can know righteousness, joy, and peace (Rom. 14:17). Jesus said, speaking of man's spirit, "He that believeth on me as the scripture hath said, out of his belly [innermost being] shall flow rivers of living water" (John 7:38).

Our soul includes our mind, our emotions, and our will. This is our Adamic nature, our *psyche,* our self. If we follow our mind, we will go to hell. If we follow our emotions, we will go to hell. The same is true if we follow our will. These three parts of what we call man's soul must be tamed and harnessed by the spirit. Paul often spoke of the conflicts between the spirit and the soul, the spirit and the flesh. It is the spiritual nature in man that must rule—and then we can cope with anything life brings our way. Then we can *live free*.

With this in mind, I invite you to explore the areas of discussion in the following pages. The idea for this book came while I was flying from Indiana to New York. I began thinking of the numerous books that deal with how to cook, how to sew, how to be a mechanic, how to be an engineer, how to be a pilot, how to be a carpenter, and many more. But I had not seen a Christian book on how to handle one's own personality. From that thought, the idea was born for a series of television programs dealing with "How to Cope." For more than a year on my program, *Today With Lester Sumrall*, I addressed subjects such as appear in this volume. Included here are several of the most widely applicable and universally vital topics from that series. My prayer is that you will find these studies inspiring, practical, and helpful in your daily walk with God and your fellow man.

This book was made possible, practically speaking, through the loving help of my dear wife and lifetime partner, Louise, who typed most of the transcripts. Also, to my church, The Christian Center of South Bend, Indiana, goes a debt of thanks for continual prayer and encouragement.

Lastly, to God be the glory and all of the praise. It is our Lord who enables us to react positively, regardless of what happens to us.

---

[1]"Psychiatry on the Couch," *Time* (April 2, 1979), pp. 74–82.

[2]"Coping Is Up to You," *The Courier News*, Bridgewater, N.J., (July 10, 1978).

1
Making Peace With Stress

This is the age
Of the half-read page
And the quick hash
And the mad dash
The bright night
With the nerves tight
The plane hop
With the brief stop
The lamp tan
In a short span
The Big Shot
In a good spot
And the brain strain
And the heart pain
And the cat nap
Till the spring snaps
And the fun's done.

—Virginia Brasier[1]

What a fitting description of today. This bit of verse, which seems so appropriate to our day, first appeared in the *Satur-*

day Evening Post in May, 1949. It is safe to say our world has become much more tension-filled in thirty years.

Everyone faces pressure of some sort. According to Dr. Hans Selye, "Stress is part of the human condition . . . the only way to avoid stress completely is to be dead."[2]

A friend was on an American Airlines DC-10 flying to Chicago during the winter of 1979. A January blizzard had dumped twenty inches of snow on the already snowbound Chicago area, and for ten-and-a-half hours he and more than a hundred other passengers were in the air (counting time for a refueling stop) on a flight that normally takes less than two hours. O'Hare Airport was operating at minimal capacity. The pilot informed the passengers that he was in a holding pattern with twelve other aircraft. There were five such holding patterns, each with thirteen planes, all being monitored for landings at O'Hare. Imagine the tension that the pilots, flight attendants, passengers, and traffic controllers experienced during that time.

Stress results even from positive events such as marriage, the birth of a baby, retirement, a change in financial state, a change of jobs, a promotion, an outstanding personal achievement, a new home, a vacation, even Christmas!

In 1967, Thomas H. Holmes and Richard H. Rahe introduced to science the "Social Readjustment Rating Scale" which consists of forty-three "life change" events, each with a point value assigned to it. Research has shown that the more points a person accumulates within a specified period, the more likely he is to contract a disease.[3]

"Modern stress comes from the inability to adapt to our surroundings and the demands of work or family. It can also come from setting up for ourselves standards which are unrealistic—impossible to attain. . . . Stress is often associated with the jobs of high-powered executives and professionals."[4]

The competitive pursuit of wealth and prestige can overwhelm and consume a person. His work drives him to strive for the promotion, to seek the extra money that comes with overtime, and to defeat the competition. Exterior rather than inner pressures often motivate such people, who feel they must "keep up with the Joneses" or "do them one better."

Some find themselves in positions where the demands are overwhelming. They are responsible for the welfare and productivity of those under them. For some, this responsibility is fulfilling; for others, it is frightening.

Stress can be caused by countless factors: poverty, owning one's own business, attending school while trying to hold down a job, poor health or major illness, having only one parent, inadequate housing, handicapped persons in the home, and frequent moves. There is the stress of interpersonal relationships with spouse, parents, in-laws, coworkers, employers, and teachers.

Stress may manifest itself physically in hypertension (high blood pressure). "Hyper" means "over," so the name describes itself: "overly tense." Continual high blood pressure can lead to stroke and heart attack. Dr. James Hassett, assistant professor of psychology at Boston University, reminds us that one in three adult Americans (46 million people) have high blood pressure. Only half of these adults know it, one reason why hypertension, a condition of continued high blood pressure, is the "silent killer." (It should be said, however, that there are some pathological causes of hypertension in which stress has no bearing.)

Most of us would answer "no" almost immediately to the question, "Are you hypertensive?" We are quick to deny that anything is really bothering us. A great number of Christians are unwilling to admit that something may be bubbling a little too high in their boilers. They reason that somehow believers are immune to ordinary pressures and strains, but by repressing their true frustrations, they only aggravate unhealthy conditions.

13

Among the realities we must learn to cope with is tension. As certain as taxes, aging, and death, tension is a characteristic of life.

No matter what career a person chooses today, tension is bound to be a part of it. If you are a production manager in a printing firm, you are constantly living with deadlines. Teachers face stress in their classes. Secretaries are under pressure to produce faster and more efficiently. Salesmen are under stress to meet their sales projections.

Physical conditions that may result from stress are muscle spasms, diarrhea, insomnia, diverticulitis, ulcers, diabetes, backaches, and migraine headaches.

People react to stress in many ways, depending on the intensity of their situations. Some try to run away from their problems by getting divorces, moving, leaving home, getting married, alienating themselves from family members, changing jobs, dropping out of school, living as hermits, abusing drugs and alcohol, and suicide.

The term "drug abuse" usually suggests the use of "street" drugs, such as heroin, cocaine, "angel dust," marijuana, and hashish. But drugs such as those found in some tranquilizers, weight-reducing pills, cough medicines, and allergy medicines are no less addictive, even if they are socially acceptable. "A drug abuser is someone— anyone—who is hooked on something that makes him feel better than he felt before he took it."[5]

For millions, the answer to excess stress lies in a drug that's become a household word: Valium (a tranquilizer). . . . Valium is the most widely prescribed drug in the country, with the number of prescriptions written yearly running at a rate of slightly less than fifty million, including refills, according to industry sources.[6]

Many persons pride themselves that they are not dependent on tension-easing drugs, and yet they are hooked on

14

alcohol. Teenagers are becoming alcoholics at an alarming rate. "Many young people have been frightened off hard drugs, which were the 'in' thing in the late sixties and early seventies, and have turned to beer and hard liquor."[7]

People under pressure often see no way out. They sometimes vent their frustrations through aggressive behavior—suicide, murder, assault and battery, and abuse of spouse and children. The pressure they feel usually does not originate with those who are the unfortunate recipients of the aggressive behavior. The balance is tipped by the stress added to what is already an "over-stress" situation. A fitting example of a person unable to handle stress was Freddie Prinze, a comedian and television star who had "everything." But the pressures of stardom overwhelmed him, and the final pressure, a contract he could not get out of, was more than he could live with. Unable to cope, he voided the contract with a bullet in his own temple.

Suicide is becoming an increasingly popular way of escape.

Each year some four thousand American teenagers turn to suicide as the ultimate means of changing their unhappy lives. And many more try it and fail. In fact, next to accidents and homicides, suicide claims more young lives in this country than anything else. . . . Pressure of one kind or another is at the root of more teenage suicides, studies show. For some, that pressure is applied by something as trivial as a case of acne that the youngster feels makes him or her unattractive; for others it is as complex as the need to be loved by a pair of warring parents.[8]

For some teenagers academic pressure is a major contributor to the suicidal impulse. When a child whose entire life revolves around scholastic achievement can withstand the pressure no longer, he looks for a way out.

Inevitably we come face-to-face with tension, stress, pressure. As with a trick candle, we may try to "blow out" the stresses of life, yet they always seem to be rekindled in our lives. To rid ourselves of overwhelming pressure, we must learn to make peace with stress.

God's Peace

To make peace with stress, we must know personally the Prince of Peace, Jesus Christ (Isa. 9:6).

Therefore being justified by faith, we have peace with God through our Lord Jesus Christ (Rom. 5:1).

Be careful for nothing; but in every thing by prayer and supplication with thanksgiving let your requests be made known unto God. And the peace of God, which passeth all understanding, shall keep your hearts and minds through Christ Jesus (Phil. 4:6,7).

Thou wilt keep him in perfect peace, whose mind is stayed on thee: because he trusteth in thee (Isa. 26:3).

Great peace have they which love thy law: and nothing shall offend them (Ps. 119:165).

These verses show God's way of coping with stress: (1) Become a believer. (2) Don't worry about anything. (3) Pray about everything. (4) Give thanks. (5) Meditate. (6) Trust God. (7) Honor God's laws.

Become a Believer

We are born anew into the family of God when we accept by faith what Jesus did for us individually when He died on the cross and arose in power and victory. That is the first step in the search for help. But what if a person already is a Christian and finds himself unable to cope with stress?

That is a valid question. I have studied life and the gracious art of Christian living. I've discovered that breakdowns rarely have anything to do with work; they have instead to do with our emotions and how we respond to those things that

16

confront us. What is keeping us from responding well to tension-filled situations? Could it be that we are keeping our eyes on the problems rather than on the Problemsolver?

Some have never acquired the habit of constant communication with their Creator through prayer. Prayer is a two-way street; we make our requests known, but we need to spend time listening to God's answers. He responds to us inasmuch as we open ourselves to receive from Him. We are spiritual paupers. Our poverty shows in our restless attempts to solve our problems and in the stress and tension we feel. We fail to take advantage of the help God has already supplied through His Word.

"You mean to tell me the Bible is going to tell me how to cope with a difficult superior in the company?" a harried businessman might ask. Yes, would be my answer. The Bible is going to tell you what some of the attributes of the individual who relies on God are. Ever heard of long-suffering? Patience? Kindness? Joy in tribulation? Do you know the meaning of Romans 12?

The believer has resources the nonbeliever knows nothing about. Our ability to cope is related directly to our knowledge of the Word of God and to our willingness to put into practice what we read there.

Don't Worry About Anything

Therefore I say unto you, Take no thought for your life, what ye shall eat, or what ye shall drink; nor yet for your body, what ye shall put on. Is not the life more than meat, and the body than raiment? Behold the fowls of the air: for they sow not, neither do they reap, nor gather into barns; yet your heavenly Father feedeth them. Are ye not much better than they? Which of you by taking thought can add one cubit unto his stature? And why take ye thought for raiment? Consider the lilies of the field, how they grow; they toil not, neither do they spin: And yet I say unto you, That even Solomon in all his glory was not arrayed like one of these. Wherefore, if God so clothe the grass of the field, which to day is, and to morrow is cast into the oven, shall he not much more clothe you, O ye of little faith? Therefore take no thought, saying, What shall we eat? or, What shall we drink? or, Wherewithal shall we be clothed? (For after all these things do the Gentiles seek:) for your heavenly Father knoweth that ye have need of all these things.. But seek ye first the kingdom of God, and his righteousness; and all these things shall be added unto you. Take therefore no thought for the morrow: for the morrow shall take thought for the things of itself. Sufficient unto the day is the evil thereof (Matt. 6:25–34).

To alter an insurance company motto, "You are in good hands with God." Trust Him!

There are practical ways to alleviate tension caused by worry. Try doing one thing at a time. I have found that by giving all my attention to what is before me, I can deal more effectively with it, without borrowing concern from other matters. In this way, I am not preoccupied and can give fully of myself in each area of life.

Another way not to worry is to enjoy what you do. "And whatsoever ye do, do it heartily, as to the Lord, and not unto men" (Col. 3:23). That is the key to thwarting every pressure we feel—do everything as unto the Lord.

The following are more "worry prevention" techniques:

Organize. The key to having a well-ordered life is organization. If you need to make lists, then make them. Make a list of long-range goals—paint the living room, term paper due, board of directors meeting, vacation plans, buy new fall suit, etc.

Another helpful list is a "need" list. This can be beneficial in the home or at work. Put a piece of paper in a convenient place with a pencil nearby. When you are nearly out of a household item or food staple, make note of it.

For times of stress that are a part of life—a performance before an audience, delivery of a speech, teaching, participation in a competition, the taking of a test, the trips to and from work—prepare yourself to the best of your ability. If you know that you must be at a certain destination at nine o'clock, you must prepare yourself about twelve hours before with clothes ready and laid out, the alarm checked and ready to ring, enough time allowed to dress and eat breakfast, gas in the car, and tickets for plane, bus, or train in hand. Tension builds if we are hurried and notice the car has no gas or if we get to the airport without the plane ticket.

Set priorities. There may come a time when we need to ask ourselves if tension-induced worries are really necessary.

Martha was busily preparing for her dinner guest, Jesus. It seemed to Martha that Mary, her sister, had forsaken her responsibilities in preparing for the occasion. It was Martha to whom Jesus lovingly addressed Himself, ". . . Martha, Martha, thou art careful and troubled about many things: But one thing is needful: and Mary hath chosen that good part, which shall not be taken away from her" (Luke 10:41,42). Then Jesus went on to explain that the one *necessary* thing was not food, but fellowship with Christ. This is what Mary had chosen. How easy it is to become "careful and troubled about many things"! They may be *good* things, but not "needful." The "needful" is your first priority. It supercedes all else, no matter how desirable other things appear.[9]

Setting priorities also involves your philosophy of life. Is your purpose in life to minister to people or to finish what is before you? If your purpose is to minister to people, then people will be a top priority in your life. What you are working on, although important, can be put aside for a time in order for you to give your *undivided* attention to the person who needs you. This means there will be no side-glances at reading material or work on your desk, or mumbles and unrelated statements that reveal your preoccupation with other matters.

When we begin to feel this way about "people" interruptions, then we need not feel "I didn't accomplish anything today." If your purpose in life is to minister to people, then you have accomplished your purpose. The corporate executive need not come to the end of a hectic day full of interruptions and unexpected (and unwelcome) phone calls, and tiredly complain, "It's been a lost day. . . ."

Know your pressure capacity. A four-year-old boy cannot bear the burden of his older brother's backpack. Each of us has physical and emotional limits. If you find life to be burdensome, then you must find ways to ease that load. Delegate to others some of your responsibilities. Eliminate some of the load. Give a "lift" to your environment to make your tasks more enjoyable. Find ways to work off your frustrations; don't waste your energies in fussing and complaining. Seek creative outlets for utilizing your talents. Ask others for ideas and help. The Bible says, for good reason, that we are to bear one another's burdens. The Lord never intended for life to be a burden.

We can learn from others. A lawyer tells me that he makes tension and worry work for him when he is arguing a case in court. He says if he were not tensed up, if he were too relaxed when he went into the courtroom, he would lose every case. Some tension is necessary for achievement. It should not be our constant state, but it is a part of our emotional makeup. However, an athletic team that stays tensed up will make stupid mistakes. A lawyer who remains uptight will not win his case in court.

The same is true in my own case. I am under pressure when I am waiting to go on television. Critical timing is involved. An unseen audience who have many needs, who are facing crisis situations, who have much at stake, await me. How will I address myself to all those unknowns? Once the program begins, I relax with that unseen audience. I am comfortable, unruffled by the bright lights, the signals being flashed at me, and the movement of the cameramen and a dozen other people off camera. My thoughts are on the viewers. I am coping with the pressure. And so can you in your situation.

Evaluate your attitudes. Worry tainted with pessimism breeds depression. Self-pity, self-centeredness, and a "doomsday" attitude back us into a corner. We fall under the pressure of "Woe is me. Nothing is working out. My whole world is crashing in on me. What am I going to do?" As we wring our hands and pace the floor, we wait for the worst. And it usually comes. Our attitude is an open invitation to the enemy of our souls to make havoc of our lives.

Our God is the God of joy. ". . . In thy presence is fulness of joy. . . ." (Ps. 16:11). He tells us, "Rejoice evermore" (1 Thess. 5:16). "These things have I spoken unto you, that my joy might remain in you, and that your joy might be full" (John 15:11). Enjoy the good things that are in your life. Don't be anxious about the stresses of life. "Cast . . . all your care upon him; for he careth for you" (1 Pet. 5:7).

Perhaps you are thinking: What "good things" are in my life? Granted, you may be facing seemingly insurmountable problems caused by physical limitations, financial burdens, wayward children, *ad infinitum.* Try adding up the plusses—you are alive, you have intelligence, and most important, you have the Lord. What are your other assets? "Count your blessings, name them one by one," as the old hymn advises. It might surprise you what the Lord has already done. The right attitude is a giant step toward coping.

Procrastination can cause tension. Often we have something that needs to be done, and we expend more energy putting it off than it would take to do it. We begin to feel the pressure of this "something" hanging over us. Next time start writing that term paper as soon as you know about it. Repair "whatever" as soon as you realize it needs repair. (This also applies to relationships.)

Ask yourself some questions: *What* is contributing to my defeated attitude? *Who* is contributing to my feelings of inad-

21

equacy (despair, discouragement—whatever your particular feelings are at this juncture)? Am I overreacting to what's confronting me? If so, why? Have I neglected counsel? "Where no counsel is, the people fall: but in the multitude of counsellors there is safety" (Prov. 11:14). Who is my real enemy? (Read 1 Pet. 5:8.)

Change what you can. Some situations causing tension in your life can be altered.

Boredom caused by too little to do or by inadequate use of one's abilities can build into tremendous tension. You can determine, by your own sense of challenge, your known abilities, and even by aptitude tests, if the position you hold utilizes your full potential. *You can* relieve the tension in your life. Change what can be changed.

Of course, be willing and ready to face the consequences when you make changes. If you are in a financially unstable position, now would not be the time to switch jobs.

A friend tells how she goes home from work at night and resigns from her position. The point is, she resigns at home within the privacy of her own four walls, out of reach of her employer, who might take her seriously. She vents her frustrations, talks to the walls, then goes back to work the next day and is able to cope. She hasn't changed her role, but she has changed her attitude. "Some degree of frustration is inevitable," she wisely states. "There are some things I can do to bring about change for the greater good of everyone. I will conscientiously work to do that."

There are times when you must stand up for your convictions. This might result in changes you hadn't anticipated or in changes you had hoped to avoid. If living with your conscience and according to biblical directives is important to you, then be willing to cope with the consequences. You can be sure that God is for you, even if man is against you, when it comes to choosing right instead of wrong. The Christian stakes his actions on the Word.

Try to anticipate stressful situations. If you must drive your car some distance from your home, for whatever reason, anticipate any stressful situation you may encounter and prepare for it before you leave home. Is you car in good running order? Do you have plenty of gas? Do you have your driver's license, house keys, and a map? Do you have the address and phone number of your destination? Do you know how to get there? Will you need to drive on expressways? If so, do you know what entrance and exit roads you need? Do you have change for tolls?

This is only one of the situations that can be made less stressful through anticipation and preparation.

Granted, there are some situations you can never predict—unexpected illness or death in the family, for instance. But have you taken care of your insurance needs? If such an emergency should arise, how prepared would you be?

A young father-to-be resigned his high-paying job that provided excellent hospital benefits within weeks of his baby's birth. When confronted with the hospital and doctor's bills of over a thousand dollars, he was astonished. Certainly he should have realized that the services of a hospital and of a trained physician cost money. Frequently we bring unneeded stress into our lives by failing to anticipate stressful situations.

Winter is approaching, and you know you should put antifreeze in your car. You procrastinate. One morning you wake up to find the ground white with snow. "Oh, no," you groan, "I didn't get the antifreeze in." Your worst suspicions are realized when you check your car.

You cannot know when natural disaster may strike, but you can know that if you buy a home alongside a river, in a low part of the city, you are inviting disaster. The house may be priced low, but is it really such a good buy?

Sometimes we are our own worst enemies. As a friend

says, "Often we aren't 'clinking thearly.' " To be prepared is to be forearmed. Preparation goes a long way toward alleviating stress.

Pray About Everything

Prayer is man's way to commune with his God. It is an effective means of relieving tension.

"Evening, and morning, and at noon, will I pray, and cry aloud: and he shall hear my voice" (Ps. 55:17). "Cast thy burden upon the Lord, and he shall sustain thee: he shall never suffer the righteous to be moved" (Ps. 55:22). "Pray without ceasing" (1 Thess. 5:17). How can we go about our daily lives praying?

One housewife tells how she prays much of the time. As she gets out of the car at the supermarket, she prays, "Lord, this is all the money we have to buy these things on the list. You will have to perform a small miracle for us to get the items we need this week." Inside the store, she talks to Him, "Lord, I had planned to have chicken this week, but they don't look very fresh and that is really too much money to pay. Show me what You think would be good to have this week instead of chicken." Then she notices fish is a special price and gets enough for her family of six.

Arnold Prater, in his revealing book *You Can Pray as You Ought,* maintains that what you believe about God is revealed by what you believe about prayer. Do you believe that God is in the house-selling business, the who-to-marry business, the what-shall-I-do-with-my-life business? Prater does, and some of the rest of us do. God can be involved in our day-to-day decision making. Prater warns that real praying can't come from the top of one's head; it's got to be from the bottom of one's heart.

That's the kind of praying that produces results. Not that we are trying to persuade God to do things our way, but we are opening ourselves up to allow Him to do what is best for us. His is an all-seeing eye. On the basis of this, you and I will never be cheated out of anything that is for our ultimate good.

Give Thanks

We can be thankful in our hearts, but few will know it. When we *give* thanks, we are showing our thankfulness through positive action.

There is much controversy and uncertainty about the words found in 1 Thessalonians 5:18: "In every thing give thanks: for this is the will of God in Christ Jesus concerning you."

Give thanks when my heart is breaking? Give thanks when my health is failing? Give thanks when my bank account reads almost zero? Give thanks when I lose my job?

What do those words in 1 Thessalonians mean? Are we to thank God for dismal circumstances? Or are we to thank God for something else—Himself, for instance? What greater cause for thanksgiving is there than that?

God is in the business of turning apparent defeat into victory. What in all of history seemed more tragic than Christ's death on the cross? Prater says, "When you can walk up to the worst thing that can happen—the cross—and turn it into the best thing that ever happened, I say that's some kind of victory!"[10]

Many of God's people have testified that they found God's faithfulness to them in their times of greatest trouble to be profound reason for gratitude. Without those particular "deep water" experiences, they might have been deprived of the greater blessing of trusting God in the face of the unknown. When we must stretch our faith to the utmost, then we will know what 1 Thessalonians 5:18 really means.

Remember, God doesn't want His children to suffer any

25

more than you, as a loving parent, want your children to feel needless pain. What God wants from us is our willingness to say, "It's all right, Lord, I know You are in control. I recognize that it is Your will that I give thanks just because You are You. I trust You to bring ultimate good out of this in some way."

Praying in that way can relieve tension, as you are able to make peace with whatever is causing you such stress.

Furthermore, we are instructed ". . . in every thing by prayer and supplication with thanksgiving let your requests be made known unto God" (Phil. 4:6).

Does that pose any problem for you? It does for some. At the same time we are making requests of God, we are giving Him thanks. Don't you usually thank someone for something *after* you've received the gift? "God, are You sure that's what You mean—I am to thank You as I ask You for things?"

This seems to indicate that the faith we exercise in giving thanks *before* requests are granted releases the peace of God. Faith is indicative of trust we place in God. "But," you say, "what if my request isn't answered the way I meant it to be; what if I thank Him, and it doesn't work out as I had hoped?"

When you thank Him that way are you hoping to bribe Him into giving you your way? Or are you thanking Him for answering your prayer in the way that He knows is best for you and everyone else concerned? That's real gratitude. When you pray, you do not worry; when you worry, you do not pray. Those are more than mere words. Help *is* just a prayer away.

Meditate

Meditation is one of the most effective methods of reducing tension in the world today. Transcendental Meditation and yoga are the most familiar types. "Simply put, meditation is a disciplined attempt to focus on one object or activity to the exclusion of everything else."[11]

Thousands of years ago, Jehovah directed His people to meditate on the book of the law—the Word of God. "This book of the law shall not depart out of thy mouth; but thou shalt meditate therein day and night . . . (Josh. 1:8). ". . . I meditate on all thy works . . . (Ps. 143:5). "But his delight is in the law of the Lord; and in his law doth he meditate day and night" (Ps. 1:2).

Frequently a mantra—the repetition of a phrase—is used in meditation to train one's thoughts not to wander.

A Christian's meditation need not consist of "vain repetitions" (Matt. 6:7). We have specific instructions for meditating on the Word of God. What sets biblical meditation apart from secular meditation is that the Word of God is alive. Meditating on the Word of God does for our spirits what food does for our bodies. The Word is assimilated into us and makes us grow.

If we are meditating, we have no time for worrying.

. . . Whatsoever things are true, whatsoever things are honest, whatsoever things are just, whatsoever things are pure, whatsoever things are lovely, whatsoever things are of good report; if there be any virtue, and if there be any praise, think on these things. Those things, which ye have both learned, and received, and heard, and seen in me, do: and the God of peace shall be with you (Phil. 4:8,9).

Excellent daily devotional books exist, which many people use regularly. A few of the best include the classic *Streams in the Desert* by Mrs. Charles Cowman, *My Utmost For His Highest* by Oswald Chambers, and *Edges of His Ways* by Amy Carmichael.

You should be reading Christian books regularly. Does your church have a library? Are you using it? Do you have a

local Christian bookstore? Do you visit there? Do you sub-
scribe to Christian magazines such as *Eternity, Christianity
Today, Charisma, Christian Life, Moody Monthly,* and
others? What are you doing to help yourself mature spiritually? If you are to live free from tension, then you need to
fortify the inner man. Christian literature can help accomplish that. Meditate on and pray about what you read;
ask God to help you put into practice what you learn. It has
been said that among the greatest ministries God has given to
men are Christian books. A book is an extension of its author,
and through the pages of Christian books you can walk with
Christian men and women. Your life will be greatly enriched
if you take the time to meditate.

Trust God

Over and over again, the Bible emphasizes the need to trust
God. We have already seen in Philippians 4:6,7 that the peace
of God comes as we keep our thoughts and hearts quiet and at
rest through trusting Him. This same message is contained in
Isaiah 26:3: "Thou wilt keep him in perfect peace, whose
mind is stayed on thee: because he trusteth in thee."

Consider these questions. In whom do you trust? In what
do you trust?

Examine your answers, and you may discover why you are
not free from stress.

Trust in riches, and see what happens. Ask the man or
woman who remembers the Depression of the thirties. Better
still, ask those who are trying to live today off what they
earmarked for retirement years ago. "He that trusteth in his
riches shall fall: but the righteous shall flourish as a branch"
(Prov. 11:28).

Trust only in people, and see how fallible they are. The
apostle Peter knew what he was talking about when he said

we should trust ourselves only to the God who made us, for He will never fail us (1 Pet. 4:19).

Trusting doesn't always come easily; we prefer to depend on the tangible rather than on that which we cannot feel or see. Often our trust in God only extends to a certain point, then we revert to elementary panic prayers. In truth, we get to our wit's end, and our actions betray our lack of trust.

When the water is calm, and the boat is rocking gently, we sail along trusting Jesus every day, as the hymn so aptly puts it. When the storms break around and upon us, we instantly reveal upon whom we rely. Trusting, I repeat, does not come easily. The apostle Peter is a case in point (Matt. 14:24–33).

Obvious answers are not always given. God's silences are full of meaning. Remember Mary and Martha waiting impatiently for Jesus to come to the side of their sick brother? Jesus waited two days before responding. When He did respond, according to the sisters' reckoning of events, it was too late. The lesson for us is: God's timetable does not always run concurrently with ours.

The hymnwriter was right:

> Trust and obey, for there's no other way,
> To be happy in Jesus, but to trust and obey.

Honor God's Laws

"O that thou hadst hearkened to my commandments! then had thy peace been as a river and thy righteousness as the waves of the sea" (Isa. 48:18).

Our generation has not honored at least one of the Ten Commandments:

But the seventh day is the sabbath of the Lord thy God: in it thou shalt not do any work, thou, nor thy son, nor thy daughter, thy

29

manservant, nor thy maidservant, nor thy cattle, nor thy stranger that is within thy gates: For in six days the Lord made heaven and earth, the sea, and all that in them is, and rested the seventh day: wherefore the Lord blessed the sabbath day, and hallowed it (Exod. 20:10,11).

The breaking of this commandment has caused needless stress in our lives.

Man is coming apart at the seams, physically and mentally, by going "full speed ahead." Because man does not honor the Lord's day, businesses are open and some employees must work. They are prevented from observing this day of God-ordained rest. There is no renewal of the spirit for the weary.

God has instructed us to be conformed to Christ, to become more like Him. To be conformed means to be shaped into the desired form (Rom. 8:29 and Phil. 3:10). We bring a lot of tension into our lives when we try to live our lives according to others' standards. When we admire someone, we seek to pattern our life after his, or we succumb to the demands of others to live our lives as *they* wish us to live. In either situation we are not honoring God's desire that we be like Christ.

I beseech you therefore, brethren, by the mercies of God, that ye present your bodies a living sacrifice, holy, acceptable unto God, which is your reasonable service (Rom. 12:1).

What? know ye not that your body is the temple of the Holy Ghost which is in you, which ye have of God, and ye are not your own? For ye are bought with a price: therefore glorify God in your body, and in your spirit, which are God's (1 Cor. 6:19,20).

Man often treats his body any way he pleases, not realizing that the body he is abusing really doesn't belong to him.

We can begin to glorify God in our bodies by eliminating

everything we know is not contributing to good health. Some researchers believe that chemical preservatives and additives in our food cause physical and mental illness. Holistic living, with an emphasis on honoring God's laws, is in order.

Holistic health is a way of life that puts you in touch with nature and yourself. Though each person's approach is different, many enjoy exercise and good natural foods.[12]

Holistic theory is a philosophical attitude, not a discipline, that views a person's health in the context of his total environment. It is the quality of total well-being. Western medicine stresses physics, chemistry and anatomy, whereas these alternate systems include consideration of family and community, religion and emotions.[13]

You should make exercise, vitamins, and techniques for relaxation work for you. In other words, just because the whole world is jogging doesn't mean that you must jog. Perhaps a brisk daily walk better fits your needs.

When the daily pressure begins to mount and you feel like screaming, take advantage of the safety valve you know works for you. For the person outside the home, eating lunch in the park may be the answer. For the housewife, lying flat on the floor listening to soothing music may be restorative.

Another major ingredient in easing stress is laughter. "A merry heart doeth good like a medicine . . ." (Prov. 17:22). "A merry heart maketh a cheerful countenance . . ." (Prov. 15:13). ". . . He that is of a merry heart hath a continual feast" (Prov. 15:15).

A television news story in 1978 featured a middled-aged man whose doctor informed him he had developed a terminal type of arthritis. Instead of accepting his fate and sitting around waiting to die, he began to seek every scanty bit of information available about his particular disease.

He found that his malady was induced by extreme stress. While he was hospitalized for treatment, he started working to reverse all the stress that had brought him to his present

31

condition. He had projection equipment brought in, and each evening, fifteen minutes before bedtime, he viewed an old slapstick humor movie—Groucho Marx, Laurel and Hardy, The Three Stooges, or Charlie Chaplin. He completely abandoned himself to laughter.

After a week he began to notice that it was later and later in the night that he had to request something for pain. Soon he needed hospital care less and less, so he moved to a hotel room, but continued with his routine, adding the comedy on television. He also began to take megadoses of Vitamin C.

Today he is completely recovered. He is known as "The Man Who Laughed Himself to Life."

To honor God's laws requires a certain discipline. It may mean parting company with those who are stumbling blocks to our efforts to live free from stress. It may mean taking a strong stand for what we are discovering to be God's will. It will surely mean loving as Christ loves.

The lovelessness that so characterizes our world is the root cause of much of our stress. We have ignored the clear teachings of the Word, we have failed to honor God's commands, and in violating these principles we have erred greatly. The consequences are stress, alienation, and difficulties in interpersonal relationships. Read 1 John 4:8–21; Romans 12:10; Hebrews 13:1; and John 13:35.

Our lives should be exhibits of the grace of God at work in the inner man. The Christian who is unable to handle stress is a poor example of the indwelling power of the Holy Spirit.

But the fruit of the Spirit is love, joy, peace, longsuffering, gentleness, goodness, faith, meekness, temperance: against such there is no law. . . . If we live in the Spirit, let us also walk in the Spirit (Gal. 5:22, 23, 25).

When we become believers, we receive the Holy Spirit. The quality of our Christian lives depends on how much of "us" the Holy Spirit controls. It is the Holy Spirit, not our best efforts, that produces the fruit.

In the final analysis, to make peace with stress we need to be completely saturated by the Holy Spirit. Jesus spoke to His disciples about the Holy Spirit's coming, "Peace I leave with you, my peace I give unto you: not as the world giveth, give I unto you. Let not your heart be troubled, neither let it be afraid" (John 14:27).

[1] Virginia Brasier, *The Saturday Evening Post* (May 28, 1949), p. 72.

[2] *The Ann Landers Encyclopedia A to Z* (Garden City, N.Y.: Doubleday 1978), p. 1144.

[3] Donald L. Dudley. M.D., and Elton Welke, "No. 1 Enemy to Health Is Man," *The Courier-News,* Bridgewater, N.J. (Nov. 28, 1977).

[4] *The Ann Landers Encyclopedia A to Z,* p. 1144.

[5] *Ibid.,* p. 416.

[6] Brian Sullivan, "Many Valium Users Ignorant of Drug's Effect," *The Courier News,* Bridgewater, N.J. (April 2, 1979).

[7] *The Ann Landers Encyclopedia A to Z,* p. 54.

[8] Brian Kates, "The Pied Piper Plays Danse Macabre," *The Daily News,* New York (April 1, 1979).

[9] Clyde and Ruth Narramore, *How to Handle Pressure* (Wheaton, Ill.: Tyndale, 1975), p. 4.

[10] Arnold Prater, *You Can Pray as You Ought* (Nashville, Tenn.: Thomas Nelson, 1977), p. 105.

[11] *The Ann Landers Encyclopedia A to Z,* p. 833.

[12] Robert Rodale, "Vitamins for the Spirit," *Prevention* (Oct., 1978), p. 23.

[13] Beth Witrogen, "How Folk Healers Tune Patients in to Nature's Harmony," *Prevention* (Oct.,1978), p. 142.

2
What Makes You Angry?

Is anger ever justified? If lying, cheating, cruelty, and bigotry do not make us mad, then isn't something wrong with us?

What kind of a God do we have if anger is wrong? The Bible says God is "angry with the wicked every day" (Ps. 7:11). His wrath, or anger, continually falls upon those who will not trust Him (John 3:36). Yes, wrath is as true a characteristic of God as is love.

Anger is not always bad. Perhaps it is easier for us to recognize and admit our anger if we realize that the most perfect One in all creation, in all time and space, becomes angry. Many Christians would answer no to the question, "Do you become angry?" Elizabeth Skoglund in her book, *To Anger, With Love*, remarks that when she told one man, " 'You are a very angry person,' he shouted back, 'I am *not* angry!' "[1] The model of the cool, unruffled businessman, or school teacher, or mother is held before us to suggest that anger is really very bad, and that we are childish when we show our anger.

Yet Jesus did not live without anger. Anyone reading the accounts in the Gospels of John and Matthew in which Jesus is confronted by hypocritical religionists, must admit there is anger in Jesus' words. "Woe unto you, scribes and Pharisees, hypocrites! for ye are like unto whited sepulchres. . . ." (Matt. 23:27). "Ye serpents, ye generation of vipers, how can ye escape the damnation of hell?" (Matt. 23:33).

Matthew, Mark, and John record that Jesus became incensed at what He saw in the temple in Jerusalem. Men who made their living by changing money into the coinage of the temple and selling live animals for sacrifices were doing business in God's house. The house of prayer had become a "den of thieves," and Jesus cleaned the whole mess out. A rope in his hand, He drove out the men and the animals and overturned the tables of the moneychangers. John says that the disciples, on seeing Jesus respond in this way, were reminded of an Old Testament Scripture: "Zeal for thy house will consume me" (John 2:17 RSV, a quote of Ps. 69:9).

Our Lord did not show anger when He was denied by Peter or when He was betrayed by Judas. But He did show anger with those who, in the name of God, reinterpreted the law for their own convenience and pretended by their public displays of piety to be righteous.

It does no good, but unimaginable evil, for us to try to convince ourselves that we do not become angry at times. We can move beyond recognizing anger to learning how to cope with it and how to turn it into a positive force in our lives.

We Live in an Angry World

The period of the 1960s was an angry era in America. The assassination of a president and later of two very prominent leaders—cut down when it appeared that they had much to offer—aggravated the anger latent within American society. The Vietnam War divided the nation. It was appropriate for President Nixon, when he ran for office in 1968, to admonish the nation to lower its voice. Since that time we have continued to live in an angry world. Elizabeth Skoglund says: "While anger has always characterized humankind, our society seems to have more than its share. Finding reasons for this is the first step in discovering how to handle and use anger."[2]

Causes of Anger

Skoglund lists three outstanding characteristics of our times that breed anger: frustration, rootlessness, and meaninglessness. "Frustration and anger are closely related," she says, "and the rapid change of values in our society has contributed to a general sense of frustration. People seem unsure of who they are and what they should be doing."[3]

Men and women are not sure today of their roles as husbands and wives, especially in homes where the wife works. The vast dehumanization that has come on the heels of our national production- and efficiency-oriented policies has made people feel that they are little more than numbers. Government is perceived as an unmanageable bureaucratic monster; there is a feeling that little the individual does will count for anything (indicated for example, by the low percentage of voters who turn out for elections).

Coupled with this, Skoglund says, is a

sense of rootlessness . . . partially the result of value conflict, but it is also due to the increased isolation of the individual in our society . . . we pay for companions, baby-sitters, and transportation. We even pay for someone to listen to us. . . . We shunt the aging off to institutions. We simply don't want to be involved, and so we feel lonely and again angry because pain always brings anger.[4]

Especially in our big cities does this anger manifest itself. A friend was walking down Madison Avenue in New York City one afternoon when a bearded young man caught his attention. In the midst of a throng of people crossing the street, this man was shouting in the ear of a lady who walked on, paying him no heed. The man's maneuvering brought him next to my friend, into whose ear he continued to shout—not obscenities, but just meaningless words. My friend felt very uncomfortable and remarked, "I don't know what you're talking about."

In a matter of seconds the shouting fellow quieted down. He told my friend, "I must be lonely." In vain he had tried to get the attention of other passers-by who seemed in such a hurry to get where they were going. The young man felt isolated from every other living being in that great crowd.

The widespread loss of life's meaning is to blame for much of the anger in our world today. Without a living faith in the Savior, many people feel they have no purpose in life. Boredom sets in, and some people, in order to relieve themselves of meaningless days and nights, get drunk or trip out on drugs. These responses are angry and destructive and only make matters worse.

Anger arises from our feelings, which are directly related to our sense of self-esteem. If someone tramples on your feelings, he has injured you. At that point, you have reason to become angry; what you do with your anger determines how the incident will end.

On the playground, Billy teases Johnny, and Johnny is hurt. Without thinking, he hits Billy and gives him a bloody nose. At home, Pam finds out she cannot go to a friend's house, and so she sticks out her tongue at her mother, slams the door of her bedroom, and utters hateful things under her breath.

At work, an announcement is made that the lunchroom refrigerator is to be defrosted later in the day. Al, the maintenance man, walks through the office and tells everyone to remove food from the refrigerator by the end of the lunch hour or it will be discarded. William is in a private office and doesn't hear the announcement, and further, he is tied up with work and doesn't go to the cooler for his lunch until everything has been tossed out.

Hungry and angry, William hears that the maintenance man has thrown out all of the items left in the refrigerator. He storms into Al's shop and asks for his lunch.

"I made an announcement," Al replies, obviously unconcerned. "I can't wait all day for people to clear the cooler, so I threw out what was in there." William explodes and stalks out, slamming the door behind him. This brings Al to William's office, angry enough to punch him; more ugly words ensue. Both these men, who work in a Christian office, maintain their anger until William seeks Al out, apologizes, and puts the matter behind him.

Some angry situations do not resolve themselves so neatly. A young father, Alex, finds a good job after quite a lengthy search. He and his wife start their family and make a down payment on a home. Then one day things don't go well at work and Alex angrily speaks up—which costs him his job. His anger probably was justified. But he knows now how important it is for him to control his temper.

Even worse—because it is potentially more destructive— is the type of anger that arises when a tired husband arrives at home after work, in no mood to hear how the children have misbehaved or what a rotten day his wife has had. Tiny, insignificant things are enough to touch off what looks like the beginning of World War III in some homes. Some husbands have learned to "dump" the day's garbage from work on their way home and turn their whole attention to their families. Still, wives complain that they get only the "rag's end" of their husband's days. This may mean short tempers and no sex; or, even worse, an angry mood that is not resolved before bedtime and which therefore breeds depression and illness.

This is not a very nice picture, but it accurately represents the kind of angry world in which we live. Against this backdrop God says, "Put away wrath." He says, "Cease from anger, and forsake wrath: fret not thyself in any wise to do evil" (Ps. 37:8).

Anger in the Bible

The first recorded outburst of anger in the Bible is the confrontation between God and Cain. Both Cain and Abel were told to bring a sacrifice before God, but Cain's sacrifice was not acceptable. God had desired a blood sacrifice, but Cain's attitude was "I will do as I please. I do not have to worship that way. God does not need a blood sacrifice. I will give Him turnips and cauliflower and onions; and if He doesn't like it, He can forget it."

When God would not accept Cain's sacrifice, Cain burned with rage. Instead of allowing his anger to convince him to change his attitude, he set his mind on vengeance. He murdered his brother. It could be said that the world's first murder resulted from uncontrolled anger, and that a religious dispute was at its root.

Anger in Religious Circles

Sadly, religious hatred still runs rampant in our world; over the centuries religion has contributed to murder, wars, and rebellions. We can think of the Crusades, of the Inquisition, and even of the modern revolution in Iran where religious issues have caused tempers to explode, leading to mass executions. On the positive side, a righteous indignation on the part of the eighteenth-century colonists in the New World led them to break ties with England and win their independence.

Anger within the churches and between churches is one of

the saddest spectacles in any day. What a terrible waste of manpower and energy when churches feud and members harbor resentment. A friend relates the story of Stonewall Jackson, who saw his men fighting among themselves over strategy and the war. The general is said to have jumped into the argument, stating, "Remember, gentlemen, the enemy is over there," pointing in the direction of battle.[5] How tragic for church members to fight each other while Satan gains victories over men's immortal souls.

Be Angry . . . but Sin Not!

The secret to coping with anger is not to deny its existence, but to keep it in control.

The Scripture says, "Be ye angry, and sin not: let not the sun go down upon your wrath: Neither give place to the devil" (Eph. 4: 26,27). Elizabeth Skoglund says this teaches us to "be angry" and "get over it quickly."[6] Frank B. Minirth and Paul D. Meier, authors of *Happiness Is a Choice*, advise that we need to "gain insight into whether [our] anger is appropriate or inappropriate" before doing anything. They further say that if we feel the anger is appropriate, it should be verbalized; then we should forgive "before bedtime."[7]

This passage from Ephesians first teaches what we have already concluded: that the sin is not in the anger but in how we handle it. Minirth and Meier say that inappropriate anger is that which "results when one's selfish demands are not being met [as in the case of Cain in the biblical story] . . . when one's perfectionist demands are not being satisfied . . . and that which results from suspiciousness."[8] Once we determine that our anger is appropriate—and that should require some pause before we do or say something rash—then what do we do?

Proverbs 19:11 says, "The discretion of a man deferreth his anger; and it is his glory to pass over a transgression."

The Revised Standard Version says "Good sense makes a man slow to anger. . . ." Since God is spoken of as being slow to anger (Neh. 9:17), we are in very good company if we defer our anger.

If something or someone makes you angry, stop and think about the situation. Do not blow your top. If you can, wait twenty-four hours before you react. Pray about the problem. Ask yourself, "What caused me to do what I did? What caused that person to say that?" It is not possible for you to be a wise father, a wise mother, a wise boss, a wise pilot, a wise doctor—if you explode. *Wisdom and anger are incompatible.*

Probably the most difficult time to defer anger is while raising children. The immediate reaction of an angered parent is to strike a child, but I advise parents to stop and think. In raising our three boys we sought always to pray with a child when he had disobeyed. We never spanked our sons for a first offense. We never punished them without trying to explain to them that it hurt us more than it did them. If a child can see that you love him, it makes the spanking a little easier to take and prevents rebelliousness from setting in. Another Scripture verse warns parents: ". . . do not provoke your children to anger, but bring them up in the discipline and instruction of the Lord" (Eph. 6:4 RSV).

A Soft Answer . . .

A familiar Scripture verse says, "A soft answer turneth away wrath: but grievous words stir up anger" (Prov. 15:1). The next time someone screams at you, don't scream back. Bite your tongue, and lower your voice. Your enemy will oftentimes be disarmed, and probably no violence will follow. Forgive a transgression, rather than screaming about it. Parents destroy the peace of their households by screaming at their children. If you often scream at your children it may be because you are a bully, or because you have not stopped to analyze what it is that is making you angry. You know that screaming at them will not be sufficient discipline when they are older. Learn how to calm down and face problems wisely and deliberately.

Aaron and Miriam belittled Moses, criticizing him for marrying a black woman. But Moses, who is called the meekest man, did not even answer them. When God saw that Moses was not going to reply, He called the three of them together and told them that Moses was His chosen prophet. Then He struck Miriam with leprosy. Moses, who had not expressed anger at his sister earlier, now prayed for her. And the Lord cured the leprosy after seven days.

We ought to strive for this kind of a meek spirit and try not to respond angrily in difficult situations. If we cannot keep from speaking, let our words be soft and gentle.

Give a Gift

Once while I was preaching a series of meetings, I discovered that the head deacon in the church hated me. God told me that I should hug and kiss this man, so the next night I found him in church and gave him a hug and a kiss. It was like embracing a telephone pole; he was cold and mean.

He had never spoken to me, and it turned out that he was angry with the way I preached and the way I looked. He told the pastor to get rid of me. But for three nights I went to him and hugged him and planted a kiss of Christian love on his cheek. The third night the pastor came to me and said, "You have charmed this man. He says you are the best preacher we have ever had." It could not have been so, for I was only a teenager. But a little love had changed the man.

Later I learned a verse in Proverbs that says, "a gift in secret pacifieth anger . . ." (Prov. 21:14). I gave this man the gift of love, and his anger toward me melted away. To love those who are unlovely—those who malign our good names, who show none of the fruits of the Spirit—that is a great challenge. We cannot succeed if we are harboring anger and resentment. They will curdle our spirits.

A friend tells how the difficulties she encountered in working for a Christian organization forced her to give the gift of love. An ungracious spirit hovered like an evil, unbidden, and unseen power in this organization. But she remembered what she had consistently told her children: You always win a better response with love. She was determined, with God's help, to put that into practice. Even though the situation did not change, she did have the quiet assurance from the Lord that what she was doing was what He wanted her to do. Later, God moved her into a position far removed from that situation, a place where she experienced the joy of knowing that God had done this thing for her. In her refusal to respond in anger, she reaped a rich reward from the Lord.

Vent Your Angry Feelings

It is not possible in one small chapter to deal thoroughly with such a subject as anger. There is, for instance, much to be said regarding anger and illness. Many of us will confess that sickness, especially long-lasting illness, brings on angry feelings. Often God is the subject of the sick person's anger. "Why did You let this happen to me?" he rages. Although understandable, such accusations are inappropriate and harmful. A person who is confined to bed or to a wheelchair may have a particularly difficult problem because he cannot engage in physical activity to vent his anger. A vigorous swim, a game of tennis, jogging, or weeding the garden can serve to release our pent-up emotions and redirect our perspectives so that we can resume our normal relations with our families.

An ill or aged person cannot work out his hostilities by

cleaning a room or by taking the dog for a brisk walk. If his anger is allowed to burn, it only aggravates his condition and makes him susceptible to further disease and an early grave. For both the aged and the ill, the most effective means of venting anger is through verbal communication. It is essential that a homebound person have a friend, a family member, or a roommate to whom he can talk out his feelings. Churches perform a vital service by sending sensitive members into homes for the aged to visit with older people on a regular basis. The staff members of these institutions find that many of these people who have been "put out to pasture" make significant recoveries physically, emotionally, and spiritually, when they are considered persons in their own rights and are challenged to make contributions where they are.

Elizabeth Skoglund says that at one time everything seemed to be going wrong in her life, and she vented some "rather cutting, sarcastic remarks" on a friend who happened to be in her presence. This suprised her and the friend, because it was not her usual way of handling things. As she and her friend talked, three things became apparent:

My feelings of anger were not sinful, they were normal; my lashing at my friend was wrong and required an apology; my real anger was at God and needed not so much to be confessed as to be relinquished to Him. All I could really say was, 'God, I'm angry because I'm hurt, but You may take the anger from me.' It was a hard prayer because I wanted to hang onto that anger and that was the point at which the problem became spiritual as well as psychological, not before.

Feelings of anger are not pleasant, and held on to they can be a self-destructive force. The challenge before us, therefore, no longer emerges as a need never to feel anger, but rather how to prevent its poison from damaging us and better still, how to use it as creatively and positively as possible.[9]

[1]Elizabeth Skoglund, *To Anger, With Love* (New York: Harper & Row 1977), p. 15.

[2]*Ibid.*, p. 17.

[3]*Ibid.*

[4]*Ibid.*, pp. 19–20.

[5]Helen W. Kooiman, *Forgiveness in Action* (New York: Hawthorn Books, 1974), p. 50.

[6]Skoglund, *To Anger, With Love*, p. 27.

[7]Frank B. Minirth, M.D. and Paul D. Meier, M.D., *Happiness Is a Choice* (Grand Rapids, Mich.: Baker, 1978), p. 150.

[8]*Ibid.*

[9]Skoglund, pp. 107–108.

3

Help Thou My Unbelief!

The situation was pitiful beyond description. A lad who could not speak lay doubled up in pain in the dust. Beside him, his anguished father sobbed. The boy had never been normal, he said. At times an unseen force drove him into danger, once almost drowning him, another time throwing him into the fire. His parents had tried numerous remedies, but to no avail. Sometimes their son foamed at the mouth and seemed crazy; but most of the time he just slouched in a corner, apathetic, uninterested in life around him.

Today the father had hoped that a miracle-working "rabbi" might help his son. But the rabbi had not arrived, and the rabbi's helpers could do nothing. On other occasions they had healed blind men and cast out evil spirits, but this day they seemed powerless to help his maddened son.

Into this desperate situation stepped the Rabbi, Jesus. Sensing the father's heartache, he inquired about the lad, and the father cried, "If you can do anything, have pity on us and help us."

To Jesus, the man's words were an affront, "If I can!" He responded. "All things are possible to him who believes!"

Reaching out with all the faith he could muster, the father

uttered words that are now famous: "Lord I believe; help thou mine unbelief" (Mark 9:24).

With that, Jesus showed the father what He could do—what God could do—when someone wants Him to help. He exorcised the demon and restored the boy to wholeness. The day of faith's victory, of answered prayer, had finally come.

Many in our world today believe there is no God. They ask, "How can I believe in a God when there is so much evil and suffering in the world? when my own life has been filled with misfortune? when there are so many catastrophes and tragedies—murders, rapes, floods, and earthquakes? How can you say there is a God?"

As I write these lines, the mother of a friend has died suddenly. The blow comes at what appears to be the worst of times for this friend, who is exhausted after preparing for an out-of-town business conference.

She hardly has the reserves to face the grief-filled experience in which she now finds herself. No one can explain why such things happens. They are a part of life.

Yet they are not all of life. For, at the same time my friend's mother died, news came of the surprising release of five Russian dissidents who had long been in prison. They were assembled in a Moscow prison and then whisked out of the country. Among them is Alexander Ginzburg for whom Alexander Solzhenitsyn has actively sought freedom. Also in the group is a Baptist pastor, Georgi Vins, for whom Christians in many countries have been praying. Perhaps you have joined thousands in asking for mercy in his behalf. The day of their release was also a day of rejoicing for answered prayers.

The good and the bad make up our earthly experience, and we are not always able to understand why things happen as they do. Corrie ten Boom likens life to a huge tapestry being woven on God's loom. While we are on earth, we can only see the "wrong" side of the tapestry, but when we get to heaven we shall see the pattern and understand that the painful colors lent their beauty to the whole, according to God's plan.

Job, who suffered as few men have, sought to know "why." His arguments with his Maker grew intense as he struggled with the evil that had befallen him. But toward the end of Job's experience, God asked him many questions:

Where were you when I laid the foundation of the earth? Tell me, if you have understanding. Who determined its measurements— surely you know? Or who stretched the line upon it? On what were its bases sunk, or who laid its cornerstone, when the morning stars sang together, and all the sons of God shouted for joy? . . . Have you entered into the springs of the sea, or walked in the recesses of the deep? Have the gates of death been revealed to you, or have you seen the gates of deep darkness? Have you comprehended the expanse of the earth? Declare, if you know all this . . . Has the rain a father, or who has begotten the drops of dew? From whose womb did the ice come forth, and who has given birth to the hoarfrost of heaven? . . . Can you hunt the prey for the lion, or satisfy the appetite of the young lions, when they crouch in their dens, or lie in wait in their covert? Who provides for the raven its prey, when its young ones cry to God, and wander about for lack of food? (Job 38:4-7, 16-18, 28, 29, 39-41 RSV)

The answer to all these questions is, of course, God. Belief in God can answer enough of the questions so that we can safely leave the questions we cannot answer in God's hands until we better understand, or until we go to be with Him.

There is an answer if man will receive it for the evil in the world. It is the Cross. The Founder of the universe, the Sovereign Creator, sent His only Son to earth because this part of His creation had fallen under the sway of Lucifer— Satan, the devil. A created being, Lucifer had rebelled against God and had come to earth to turn the whole human race against God (Isa. 14:12-15; Ezek. 28: 12-19). But God loved man whom He had created so much that He dispatched

49

His Son Jesus to earth to "destroy the works of the devil" (1 John 3:8). On the cross Jesus reached out both hands, gathered up all of the broken lines of man's rebellion, and "closed the circuit" in His own body, receiving the lethal dose of hell's fury in His own person. The result was His death. But the positive outworking was that in His death He drained all the energy from Satan's generators; death and sin lost their power over man. On the gladdest of days, God resurrected this same Jesus to life, to give life to all who will believe in Him.

This brings us squarely back to the issue of faith and unbelief. The Cross and the Resurrection are facts. In light of what God has done, do you see how cruel unbelief is? Unbelief steals bread from the widow and holds back water from the thirsty man. Unbelief kicks the crutches out from under the arms of the cripple. Unbelief blinds the youth and dims the eye of the aged. Unbelief creates the free thinker, the materialist, the agnostic, the atheist. It screams "No!" without thinking, without reasoning, without proving.

Rather than seek to know the reason for Jesus' death, unbelieving man cries out, ". . . If he be the King of Israel, let him now come down from the cross, and we will believe him" (Matt. 27:42). Unbelief does not try to understand why Jesus would not come down and why He could not save the human race if He saved Himself.

Nor will unbelief attribute to God the things that are obviously of Him. In the Book of Acts strange things happened when the Holy Spirit fell on the early church during the Feast of Pentecost. New believers began speaking in other tongues, arresting the attention of the entire city of Jerusalem. But even though it was only nine o'clock in the morning, the enemies of the gospel explained the wild happenings by claiming that the Christians were drunk (Acts 2:13).

When Jesus performed signs and wonders, giving sight to the blind and healing the sick and feeding five thousand persons with five loaves and two fish, there were those who rigged a devilish charge against Him. They said, "He is doing this by the power of Beelzebub, the prince of the devils." They should have known the devil is not the author of good, but they would not believe. Unbelief is so unreasonable that it sees God at work and gives Satan the credit.

Unbelief can be very selective, according to what best suits its purpose. At Pentecost, the religious leaders chalked up the Christians' unusual behavior to "too much wine," a superficial assumption. At other times, unbelief demands statistics and visible proof before it will attribute a thing to God.

Doubting Is Not Unbelief

This is not to say that we are not to ask for material evidence when our faith is weak. Thomas, one of Jesus' chosen apostles, required something more than the mere word of the other disciples who claimed they had seen Jesus and that He had risen from the dead. "Unless I see in his hands the print of the nails, and place my finger in the mark of the nails and place my hand in his side," Thomas said, "I will not believe" (John 20:25). A week later, Jesus showed Himself to the disciples and specifically invited Thomas to touch Him and examine Him. Thomas had no need. Falling on his knees, he cried, "My Lord and my God!" (v. 28).

Had Thomas refused to believe and required other evidence, then we could say that he was not merely a doubter, but an unbeliever. Doubting is not the same as unbelief. To doubt is to hesitate in judgment, to be uncertain, unsure. Doubt has its roots in the Latin word *dubitare*, akin to our English word "dubious," which means unsettled. Doubt can be a healthy reaction. We may doubt a thing is true—a healing of the body, an answer to a prayer, a statement in the Bible that seems too good to be true—but that does not mean unbelief is residing within us. Unbelief is negativism, a disposition not to believe.

Agnosticism?

What of the agnostic? By definition, this is a person who "holds the view that any ultimate reality (as God) is unknown and probably unknowable."[1] Agnosticism is unbelief in the guise of respectability and is the special pitfall of the sophisticated and the well-educated. Faced with things difficult to believe, the simpler mind will believe and wonder that others find believing so hard. They are like the robin and the sparrow in the familiar verse by an unknown poet:

> Said the robin to the sparrow,
> "I should really like to know,
> why these anxious human beings
> rush about and worry so."
> Said the sparrow to the robin,
> "Friend I think that it must be,
> that they have no heavenly Father
> such as cares for you and me."

I do not mean to criticize or make light of the agnostic. Many agnostics are far from comfortable, and they hold their position in what they think is complete honesty. They do not think it possible to take any other stance toward life. You may consider yourself an agnostic. If so, it is my prayer that you will soon be able to say, "I believe, help Thou my unbelief."

Beatrice Balletta is one who made this move. She describes her experience in this excerpt from the *Logos Journal:*

As I grew up, other interests occupied my thoughts, and by the time I reached high school, I considered the belief in a personal, conscious God, and the immortality of the soul, to be sheer nonsense. Mostly I was quite content to be living without any faith in God.

I developed a fascination for philosophy books. But following the thinking of the different philosophers was purely on the level of intellectual curiosity. Mine was no search for truth, because *the truth I already knew: it was impossible to know anything about our origin or the meaning of life, and death meant the end of everything.* Spinosa became my favorite philosopher.

Then one day, after completing one year at Hunter College, it happened: the whole wall came crashing down around me. It was like being hit with a thunderbolt.

I had been having a minor argument with my mother and thought to myself, ''Why get excited about this? A short while from now, we won't even remember what the argument was about.'' With that, I was suddenly inundated by a staggering, intense realization of the transitoriness of our whole life. If this life is all that we shall ever know, if death means the end of everything, then we are passing illusions—there is no reality. Nothing we do or think or say has any meaning. The intellectual honesty in which I prided myself would be meaningless, as would also such things as social reform and scientific advancement and cultural pursuits, and all moral values. In fact, there would be no sense to eating or sleeping or talking or sitting or standing. Then why were we born? To wait around to become nothing again, and try meanwhile to amuse and distract ourselves as best we could? That seemed to be the gist of it. We were soap bubbles in some senseless, cruel drama.

The thought of the meaninglessness and uselessness of everything was so strong and inescapable that I was filled with real terror and could not eat or sleep for days at a time. At night I would lie in bed shaking all over, in a cold sweat. And during the day, I would walk through the familiar streets of the Bronx, looking around me in amazement because everything had suddenly become so different.

My family and friends knew that something had happened to me. But I could not talk to them about the agony I was experiencing because I was sure that nobody would be able to understand. But because of their great concern for me, I forced myself when with them, to go through the motions of being my old self.

I used to spend long hours trying to reason out whether or not there was a God. But it was in vain. The more I reasoned, the less likely it seemed that I would ever be able to come to any kind of truth. I went back to the philosophy books, now with a new interest. But those philosophers and their elaborate systems seemed so empty now. . . .

I also studied the different religions of the world; and I talked with many people, including some priests. Through the latter I became familiar with the saints and Catholic philosophers. But the result of all this was a deepening sense that it was not possible for anyone to know anything about our origin and destiny.

Through all my reading and listening and thinking, however, I had formed a desire to believe in Jesus. But the more maddening this desire became, the more fiercely I fought to avoid giving in to what seemed like wishful thinking. I wanted certainty. But what could I do? I had reasoned, read, studied, talked with others. The priests I talked with were constantly telling me that they were praying for me. One day in desperation I got down on my knees and said, "God, if you exist, and can hear me, then help me. *I* can't do any more." So I had added prayer in my search.

But still there was only darkness. It seemed that I had done everything in my power, and there was no response from God. Was that the sign that he could not hear me—that he did not exist? Yet in my state of desperation, I could not just forget the whole thing.

I continued in this despairing state for a long time. Everything ceased to interest me. I could see no reason for continuing to live. But the thought that I was soon to disappear and become absolutely nothing, forever and ever, filled me with indescribable terror. And my desire to believe in a God who knows us and loves us, and who wants our love, was becoming unbearable.

Then one day it dawned on me that there was just one more thing that I could do to find out if there was a God. . . .

I went to a priest friend and asked him to baptize me. I told him that I still had no faith, but knew that if I took this one blind leap in the dark, then if there really was a God, he would have to take over and give me faith. It was the very last thing for me to do. Later I learned that just before I came to see him on that particular day, the priest had asked all the sisters in his parish to pray very specifically during the whole time of our visit.

And so the following week I was baptized. I felt no kind of exhilaration—just an inner peace, a feeling that somehow the awful battle was over. Then gradually, gently, the Lord began to reveal himself to me in many different ways; and the certainty which I had been seeking, for so long a time, did come—but in his way, not mine. God is a Person, not an idea, and we cannot arrive at a knowledge of him the way we arrive at a scientific truth. We cannot find our way to God—but God became man to find us. Faith, I learned, is a gift from God, not something we can reason our way to. We have to believe in order to understand. Very soon I reached the point where it was easier to doubt my own existence than God's."[2]

Miss Balletta's moving story continues today. Her faith grows as she renders loving service to others as a member of the Society of the Holy Child Jesus. Not all have such a difficult time receiving the gift of faith as she did. A person raised in a Bible-loving home and church may not be able to point to a time when he or she did not believe in Jesus. Such people were trusting Jesus even when they were children. But such persons still may wrestle with unbelief. They need to practice habits that will cause their faith to grow. As C. S. Lewis said, they must "train the habit of Faith."[3]

Feed Your Faith and Starve Your Doubts

The first step in training faith and thus overcoming unbelief is to nurture faith within. You can rid yourself of unbelief by opening your heart and mind to the Word of God. Paul said it well: "So then faith cometh by hearing, and hearing by the word of God" (Rom. 10:17).

Saturate yourself in the Bible. Hearing the Word of God means going to church, unless the Bible isn't used where you attend. In that case, switch churches; your faith depends on it. Add to the public hearing of the Scriptures the habit of reading the Bible in your home. If you feed your inner man—your emotions, your mind, your soul—with the good Word of God, then faith will come into your heart, and unbelief will go. The Navigators, a Christian organization ministering on college campuses and military bases, suggests five ways we can bring the Word of God into our lives: *hearing* (which takes the least effort and is the least effective way to retain truth), *reading, studying, memorizing,* and *meditating* (which can involve much of our time and which continues to bring benefits to our lives the more we practice it). I heartily recommend that a person who wants to see his faith grow enroll in the Navigators' Topical Memory System. You can not only lay up more than one hundred carefully chosen Scripture verses in your heart, but you also learn sound principles of retaining them and learning more of your own choice.[4]

It is necessary to have a plan for reading the Bible, so that you will get the most from it. I suggest that a person begin with the Book of Romans, if he is unfamiliar with the Bible. This book will tell you what it is to be a Christian. The very first chapter of Romans will tell you where all of man's religions originated. Next, read James in order to see how to live as a Christian. Then read the Gospel of John, to see whom you love and who loves you. That done, read the New Testament through, and then turn to the Old Testament. There are plans available for reading the entire Bible in a year. Reading the Word daily, engaging with others in Bible study, and laying up some portions through memorization will enable you to meditate on the Word of God "day and night." This will qualify you for God's promised blessing, for you will ". . . be like a tree planted by the rivers of water, that bringeth forth his fruit in his season; [your] leaf also shall not wither; and whatsoever [you] doeth shall prosper" (Ps. 1:3).

Act on Your Faith

Unbelief is negative; faith is positive.

If you wish to displace unbelief, then you must act on the Word of God. When God says something, do it. The Bible is filled with examples of men and women who displaced unbelief by a positive act of faith.

Noah saved his family by building the ark. He acted on faith. It is likely he had never seen a boat. He could have said, "I have never seen a boat and don't know anything about building one." He could have doubted that it would rain long enough to flood the earth. But he didn't do those things; instead, he acted and built the ark *by faith.*

Abraham fathered a whole nation. Most of us would question how that would be possible. But Abraham believed, and he acted on what he believed.

Moses had been a shepherd in the wilderness for forty years when God said, "Moses, I will cause you to deliver a whole nation. You will go out in front of them. You will hold up the banner, and behind you will be a nation who will follow you out of Egypt and to the Promised Land." Moses tried to excuse himself, but when he finally agreed to obey, he saw that God could do the impossible. Oh, that God would put that sort of faith in our hearts today.

Joshua came to the Holy Land, and God said, "See this country? I will knock down the giants and the walled cities and everything else. Go and take it! Everywhere you put your foot, I will give you the land." Joshua said, "Thank You. I believe it." He went in and conquered the enemy. You can do it too. Conquer unbelief by an act of faith.

Principle of Faith Is Within You

I remember when a small group of Christians in London badly needed a place of worship. They had no money, but my friend Howard Carter, who was the president of a Bible college in Hampstead (north of London), told them, "I'll give you a place." He signed a contract for an empty church building, promising that in ninety days he would pay the full amount.

The students and faculty knew Mr. Carter, and they couldn't believe he had done this. When they asked if he had the money, Mr. Carter replied, "No, but I'm sure God knows where it is."

A week later they asked him again, and he merely shrugged his shoulders. "I'm not worried," he said, "God doesn't give it to me before I need it."

Two months went by, and the faculty and students of the Bible college began to be nervous. "How much of the money do you have now?" they would ask, but he would just say, "I haven't even asked for it yet." Horrified, they told him that he ought to have at least two thirds of the money by that time. "No," he said, "that is not the principle of faith. The principle of faith is within you. You know the moment you need a thing that it will be delivered to you."

On the day before the deadline, some students agreed to fast and pray. "The bank has to have that money by tomorrow," they said, almost in desperation; but Howard Carter continued about his duties. He wasn't going to fast. He was trusting God. At dinner he admitted that he didn't have a pound toward the cost of the building.

In London at that time, there were five mail deliveries a day. The last one was at 9:00 P.M. As was his habit, Howard Carter picked up the last mail delivery, took it to his quarters, and left it on the mantle. He had already gone to bed when something told him to look in the mail for a large brown envelope. He tried to shrug off the idea, but it persisted. Finally, believing the Lord was telling him to get up and look in the envelope, he crawled out of bed. Sure enough, he found a large brown envelope, and it was filled with money. Counting the bills, he saw that it was enough for the total payment that he would need the next day. No letter was inside nor was there a return address. The rain had ruined the postmark so that he could not tell where the money had come from.

The next morning at breakfast, spirits were low—except for Mr. Carter's. He was almost beside himself. Finally, he passed the envelope around and asked everyone to look inside. One by one, they expressed shock and amazement.

"When did it come?" someone asked. "Last night," he answered.

"Did you have it with you at supper?" another asked.
"No."

"Who sent it?" He did not know. But that day he went to the bank, and the church building became the property of the people to whom it had been promised three months earlier. To all concerned, it was an unforgettable example of faith in action.

God is faithful. All we need to do is believe Him when He says: ". . . Have faith in God . . . therefore I say unto you, what things soever ye desire, when ye pray, believe that ye receive them, and ye shall have them" (Mark 11:22,24).

[1]*Webster's Collegiate Dictionary.*

[2]Beatrice Balletta, "Blind Leap in the Dark," *Logos Journal* (Sept./Oct., 1978), pp. 56–58; Logos International, Plainfield, N.J., copyright 1978, used by permission.

[3]C.S. Lewis, *Mere Christianity,* (New York: Macmillan, 1942).

[4]The Navigators, Colorado Springs, Col. 80901.

4
The Guilt Trip

A young woman is caught smuggling heroin—*guilty!*

Police snatch a car thief, and he winds up behind bars—*guilty!*

A bank employee is sent to prison for embezzling—*guilty!*

A president's term is embarrassingly interrupted, brought on by accusations of guilt.

The world is full of guilty people, but the surest indicator of guilt is not the verdict of the court. Lie detectors are, at best, only ninety-three percent effective—at worst, seventy percent.[1] Juries may be fooled, but one judge—our conscience—unfailingly points the finger.

Divinely built into our being, our conscience is the harshest of judges. It hounds us day and night. We can keep things from our families, our bosses, our teachers, the police, the IRS, and almost everyone else; but only with the greatest of effort and conditioning can we train our consciences to acquit us.

As a boy growing up in Laurel, Mississippi, I recall a man who killed a local resident named Rice and threw the body into a sawmill log pond. The killer was not found until ten years later and then only because he could not escape his own conscience. A chance remark to a friend led to the discovery of the body at the bottom of the pond. Only bones and pieces of a rusty chain remained as evidence, but that was enough to convict the killer and send him to prison—all because of a guilty conscience.

Guilt—True and False

There are guilty people—and there are others who just feel guilty.

For many of us, our theological understanding isn't enough. In spite of all the assurances of our religious tutors (or perhaps because of them), we simply cannot shake that deep feeling that God disapproves of us. We sometimes have a hazy perception of God as that great dispenser of disapproval in the sky. We're sure that when we cross God's mind, he thinks, I'm OK; you're not OK.[2]

Psychiatrist Karl Menninger begins his book, *Whatever Became of Sin?,* by telling of a nameless man who stood on a busy Chicago street corner in the Loop one day in 1972. "As pedestrians hurried by on their way to lunch or business, he would solemnly lift his right arm and, pointing to the person nearest him, intone loudly the single word 'GUILTY,' " says Menninger.[3] People's responses were varied. They would look at the man, hesitate, look at one another, and then hurry on their way. One man, turning to another, exclaimed, "But how did *he* know I am guilty?"

Feelings of guilt come upon us when our conscience flashes the warning signal: You have broken one of God's laws. Yet these same guilty feelings can come over us when we are not guilty. Our conscience can become confused.

Soldiers have returned from battle deeply scarred by guilt complexes from having killed in combat. Yet they are bearing false guilt. In almost every case, they were performing their duties as defenders of their country. They have not murdered; what they did was required of them by the government. I try to tell such persons that, although the war may have been immoral, they were not there of their own will.

Similarly, we can feel a twinge of guilt at seeing someone less fortunate than we. It is not uncommon to have this sense of false guilt on seeing a person who has no legs, or who is blind, especially if the person is younger than we.

Bruno Bettelheim, the noted author and professor of psychology at the University of Chicago, survived both Dachau and Buchenwald concentration camps. According to Paul Robinson, who reviewed Bettelheim's new book *Surviving* in *The New York Times Book Review* (April 29, 1979), psychologist Bettelheim noted that he and his fellow survivors share a common guilty feeling for having survived the Holocaust. "They have an almost obsessive need to find purpose in life: Since they were granted a reprieve, their existence, they feel, must justify itself."[4]

These examples point up a principle: *You are not guilty of that for which you are not responsible.*

Satan is out to discourage and destroy you, and false guilt is one of his cleverest weapons. You must not let the past haunt you. Do as Paul said: ". . . forgetting those things which are behind, and reaching forth unto those things which are before, I press toward the mark for the prize of the high calling of God in Christ Jesus" (Phil. 3:13,14).

An older woman, who was a faithful volunteer worker in our church, walked into my office one day, urgently in need of consolation. As I listened, she spilled out a tale of sin. But it was about something she had done when she was a college girl.

"Didn't Jesus save you?" I asked her.

She said yes.

"And didn't He forgive you all your sin?"

She nodded, but added, "I cannot forget."

I told the dear woman that all she needed to do was to tell

the Lord once that she was sorry for her sin, and guilt had to go. At last she seemed to believe the good grace of her God.

We are bent on indulging our sense of failure and guilt. Instead of pounding our fists, or doing something worse to assuage our guilt, we need to hear the apostle John's words in 1 John: "If our heart condemn us, God is greater than our heart, and knoweth all things. Beloved, if our heart condemn us not, then have we confidence toward God" (3:20,21).

A second principle is: *You are not guilty of something for which you have been forgiven.*

To nurture a guilty feeling is to deny the love of God, the sacrificial death of Jesus, and a hundred promises from God's Word. Such are His promises: "As far as the east is from the west, so far hath he removed our transgressions from us" (Ps. 103:12); or, "I have blotted out . . . thy transgressions . . ." (Isa. 44:22); or, as Paul said it: "There is therefore now no condemnation to them which are in Christ Jesus, who walk not after the flesh, but after the Spirit" (Rom. 8:1).

Imagine that at this moment you are called before the judgment seat of Christ. You are swept up without warning and made to answer for the way you have lived. Standing as prosecuting attorney in front of the Great Judge is your accuser, Satan, and he names a sin which you have only recently committed. He accuses you before the angelic witnesses and a host of people whom you recognize as believers who have died and gone to heaven before you. You are totally ashamed and overcome with grief as you await the words from your Judge. But he states, "What sin? He has been forgiven. There is nothing at all against this man's account. He is washed in the blood!" That is what God means by "no condemnation."

Transgression—Then Guilt

In a moral universe such as ours, we cannot break God's

laws without being affected. Guilt radically altered life for Adam and Eve. Before they transgressed the command of the Creator, they were tranquil, guileless, and unaware of any evil desire for each other's bodies. But the moment they disobeyed, they were driven by shame into the bushes to find coverings for their naked bodies. Guilt came. Sin is the mother of guilt.

Guilt breeds *loneliness*. If you are guilty of some wrong, and you have not trained your conscience to ignore it, you are probably a person who is lonely at times. Guilt cuts you off from others; nothing symbolizes this as vividly as the steel bars of a prison. This is awful, literal loneliness. We don't have to go to jail to feel the loneliness brought on by guilt. Part of the reason a guilty person is lonely is that he does not want to be discovered. Loneliness is the price we pay when we do not risk involvement.

Guilt also breeds *despair*. A person driven by guilt will say, "What is the use of living, anyway? I am a failure. I am helpless. Everything I do fails. I will be found out." Judas despaired of his life when he saw how his greed and deceit had led to Jesus' cruel crucifixion. Seeing no more reason to live, he went out and hanged himself. If you catch yourself saying that you are no good, that you are a failure, that you would be better off dead, watch out! You may be dangerously near to committing suicide. Seek out a friend, a pastor, a counselor, the police. Let matters rest while you seek perspective. Life can improve. The Lord has not forgotten you. Simon Peter and others had reasons for despair, but their lives were changed as they passed through the crises.

Fear is a very real effect of guilt. It is so serious a problem that we devote an entire chapter in this book to the subject. A companion effect is *bitterness*.

Remember the time you bit into a piece of fruit, anticipating a sweet taste, only to discover that it was bitter! You quickly drew it from your lips. Guilt produces a similar reaction in our spirits. Guilt is a sour grape. It may not be notice-able at first, but gradually, if we do not deal with guilt, we become angry with ourselves and with others. Woe to the person who does not resolve his guilt feelings, for bitterness will separate him from the world; and loneliness, fear, and despair can drive him to suicide. Bitterness is a serious prob-lem. Solomon said, "The heart knoweth his own bitterness . . ." (Prov. 14:10). Paul commanded: "Let all bitterness, and wrath, and anger . . . be put away from you . . ." (Eph. 4:31).

Along with these four effects, there are definite emotional responses accompanying guilt. We feel unworthy; our self-respect diminishes. Resentment toward others mounts up; we feel paranoid. We suspect others are talking behind our backs. We live more and more to ourselves, filled with regret.

In May, 1977, when former President Richard Nixon agreed to a televised interview with David Frost, I was among a host of Americans who waited to see what Mr. Nixon would say. As the interview proceeded, it became clear that the recollection of Watergate was deeply troubling to the former president. I found myself wanting the man to break clean and tell us he had done wrong. The closest thing he did was to admit that he had let the American people down. When pressed to the ropes, he often hung onto small fringes of fact, interpreting his actions in a self-serving man-ner, never admitting his guilt.

I suspect that all of us see something of ourselves in Mr. Nixon. We cannot throw stones at him, for we, too, hedge on the truth and seek to cover it up. The only way out of the dark corner is through confession of guilt. How dearly we pay for being unwilling to say, "I was wrong. I am sorry." An indi-vidual is never so big in the eyes of others as when he is willing to humble himself before God and man and admit to his wrongdoing. Humility is a virtue that never goes out of style. "Humble yourselves therefore under the mighty hand

66

of God, that he may exalt you in due time" (1 Pet. 5:6). Jesus said, "Whosoever therefore shall humble himself as this little child, the same is greatest in the kingdom of heaven" (Matt. 18:4).

You Can Be Forgiven

If we are guilty of wrongdoing, we may ask for mercy and be assured that God grants it. If we are not guilty, then we must let guilty feelings and accusations run off our backs as water runs off a duck's back. Guilt is not a thing we have to carry around with us. It is not inevitable, like advancing age and death. We can be forgiven completely. Here are four examples from the Bible. With an open mind, judge for yourself whether God can wipe away your guilt.

David

A young shepherd boy, David, became the king of Israel. A great warrior, he led Israel in defeating all her foes and in claiming much of the territory that rightfully belonged to her.

He was king of God's chosen people, a man whom the prophet Samuel had chosen out of many others to be the leader. His reign even elevated him above all of Israel's kings, so that he was an early precursor of the Messiah. Promises were made to him of an everlasting kingdom that could only find fulfillment in Jesus.

But David became soft. Once, while his armies were fighting Israel's enemies, he lusted after the beautiful wife of one of his soldiers, Uriah, whose property was adjacent to the king's palace. The story of his adultery is well known. When Bathsheba became pregnant, David brought Uriah home from the battlefield, so as to cover his sin. But when this failed, he ordered Uriah into the thick of the battle and commanded that he be left unprotected against the enemy. Uriah was killed.

King David then proceeded to live a lie, but God knew and sent his prophet to David. Nathan confronted David with his sin, and David confessed fully, deeply remorseful that he had done wrong. As a consequence, God did not allow the baby born to Bathsheba to live, although David fasted and prayed for many days. Finally, in later years, one of David's sons turned against his father. David paid for his sins many times over, but he was restored to fellowship with God early after his fall into temptation, and he recorded the happiness of being forgiven in one of his best-known psalms.

Blessed is he whose transgression is forgiven, whose sin is covered.
Blessed is the man to whom the LORD imputes no iniquity, and in whose spirit there is no deceit.
When I declared not my sin, my body wasted away through my groaning all day long.
For day and night thy hand was heavy upon me; my strength was dried up as by the heat of summer.
I acknowledged my sin to thee, and I did not hide my iniquity;
I said, "I will confess my transgressions to the LORD!"; then thou didst forgive the guilt of my sin (Ps. 32:1-4 RSV).

Peter

Consider Simon Peter. No other man was so close to Jesus, except perhaps John. Peter was the one who declared that Jesus was the Christ, "the son of the living God." He was with Jesus on the Mount of Transfiguration, and there he saw Moses and Elijah appear in glory. He was among the select group that was with Jesus when he raised Jairus' daughter from her deathbed. He walked on the water and declared that he would never, ever deny his Lord. But we know that Peter not only denied Jesus, but did it three times, loudly, and with curses.

You and I have not been physically close to Jesus, nor have we turned our backs on Him in His hour of greatest need, as did Peter. Peter, crushed with guilt, wept bitterly and re-

68

pented of his sin. Then Jesus surprised Peter by appearing to him after His resurrection to show him that all was forgiven. In a poignant encounter on the shore of Galilee (John 21), Jesus three times asked Peter if he loved Him. Peter was beautifully restored and recommissioned to the Lord's service. His guilt behind him, Peter went on to preach the sermon at Pentecost, which ushered three thousand souls into the church, and he, with Paul, did more than any other person to establish the church in the first century.

The Thief on the Cross

Two criminals were crucified with Jesus (Luke 23:32–43). They are referred to as thieves in the Gospels. One was evidently a hardened criminal who had nothing good to say about Jesus and who joined the crowd of tormentors in mocking Jesus. But the other thief said, "Look, stop talking like that. We're here because we deserve to be here. But this Man has done nothing wrong." Then he pleaded with Jesus, "Remember me, Lord, when You come into Your kingdom." Jesus did not put him off, but assured him: "To day thou shalt be with me in paradise" (Luke 23:43). The man's guilt was forever gone.

The Prodigal Son

Finally, the story of the prodigal son in Luke 15 further illustrates God's treatment of guilty sinners. The young son of a wealthy landowner took all of his inheritance and left home. He wasted his substance in "riotous living," buying for himself whatever his heart desired. He abandoned the moral teachings of his parents, fully indulging his lusts until he ended up penniless, dirty, homeless, hungry, and ashamed. The country he was in was experiencing a famine, and he was forced to take a job feeding swine. As a Hebrew, he would never under normal circumstances have eaten pork or kept swine; his condition in the parable shows that he had fallen to the lowest level possible.

The Scriptures say that he "came to his senses." He realized that none of his father's servants had to stoop so low as he had. His mind was made up; he would return home. On the way home he recited what he would say to his father.

Father, I have sinned against heaven and before thee, And am no more worthy to be called thy son: make me as one of thy hired servants (Luke 15:18,19).

But did the father accept such a suggestion? Of course not. Instead he said,

. . . Bring forth the best robe, and put it on him; and put a ring on his hand, and shoes on his feet: And bring hither the fatted calf, and kill it; and let us eat, and be merry: For this my son was dead, and is alive again; he was lost, and is found. . . (Luke 15:22–24).

Jesus told the story to show the magnitude of our heavenly Father's love. To God it does not matter how deeply into sin you have fallen. If God can forgive David, Peter, the thief on the cross, and the prodigal son, He has no trouble forgiving you and me. He loves us so much that He gave His Son for us. He is waiting for us to repent, as all four of these people did.

Guilt is not an insignificant thing; it is ugly and monstrous. We have seen that we must learn not to allow false guilt to bother us. We have seen also that we must not trust our feelings if, although God has forgiven us, we do not immediately *feel* forgiven. It is a part of our proud makeup not to forgive ourselves until we have properly endured pain for our sins. But when we entertain such thoughts, we need to return to the truth declared in Romans 8:1—"There is therefore now no condemnation to them which are in Christ Jesus, who walk not after the flesh, but after the Spirit."

[1]*U.S. News and World Report* (Mar. 8, 1978), p. 68.

[2]Gaius Berg, *Adult Teacher's Guide*, Dec./Feb., 1979–80, (Elgin, Ill.: David C. Cook Publishing Co.), pp. 69–76.

[3]Karl Menninger, *Whatever Became of Sin?* (New York: Hawthorn Books, 1973), p. 1.

[4]Paul Robinson, "Apologist for the Superego," *New York Times Book Review*, Apr. 29, 1979, p. 7.

5

Beyond the Grip of Fear

During the 1978–79 television season, one program on the series *Taxi* dealt in a humorous way with fear. It seems that Alex, a New York cabbie, had been mugged and shot. Not seriously injured, he was able to return to work a few days after the incident. But he was afraid to go back on the streets, for fear that the same thing might recur.

Alex's fellow drivers persuaded him that there was only one way to overcome this fear. He had to drive out of the station, collect a passenger, and deliver him to his destination. At first the mere idea of doing this only revived Alex's fears. But his friends persisted, and reluctantly he took to the street.

If you've ever been to New York, you know that you can hardly walk a block without seeing someone hail one of the scores of cabs on the street. Alex drove past several would-be passengers, until he thought he recognized a priest waiting for a cab. Sure enough, it was a priest, and Alex, feeling relieved, pulled over. But then his passenger asked to be taken to the pier, hardly the safest place in town at night.

"Are you sure you're a priest?" asked the doubtful driver. "You look too young to have been to seminary."

The man assured Alex that he was a priest, but Alex was

still anxious. He thought of a way to confirm that the man was a priest.

"The other day," he began, "some of us were talking about the twelve apostles of Jesus, and we couldn't remember all their names. I bet if you're a priest you know them all, don't you?"

The priest began listing them—"Peter, James, John, Andrew, Matthew, . . . er, uh, Judas . . ." then, silence. When he could go no further, Alex pulled over and made him get out, convinced that the man was not a priest.

"Fear creates what it fears," says Dr. Paul Tournier, Swiss physician and author. He points out that

stagefright inhibits speech; the fear of being like one's father or mother leads to an ever-increasing resemblance, and plays a part at least as important as true heredity; the fear of not keeping one's resolutions prevents them from being made whole-heartedly, so that failure is inevitable . . . the fear of 'cracking,' of not having strength enough for a task, saps our strength so that we do 'crack'; the fear of disappointing her fiance prevents a girl from acting naturally, so that she does disappoint him.

The fear of not being loved warps a woman's outlook, so that her husband wearies of her and becomes estranged; the fear of not being pretty enough makes her lose her good looks and impels her to disfigure herself with ridiculous make-up; the fear of growing thin stops her putting on weight; the fear of losing his wife's confidence turns a man into a dissembler, so that he arouses her mistrust; the fear of growing old makes us grow prematurely old; the fear of suffering leads us into a thousand errors which brings endless suffering in their train; the fear of penury leads us to speculations in which we lose the little we have; the fear of unemployment makes a young man change his job, so that he finishes up without one; or his fear of not being able to marry, through not having a good job, deprives him of the energy he needs to succeed in his career.[1]

These thoughtful summaries from the Swiss doctor's notebook have been confirmed in my own counseling experience. No wonder fear has been called man's deadliest enemy, for it paralyzes a human being, halting action.

The medical profession has given names to specific types of fears. There is ailurophobia—a fear of cats; algophobia—a fear of pain. There are:

androphobia	fear of or aversion to men
anemophobia	fear of winds or drafts
aphephobia	aversion to being touched by people
arachnephobia	fear of spiders
astrephobia	fear of thunderstorms
astrophobia	fear of the sky, its mystery
autophobia	fear of being alone
basiphobia	fear of walking
bathophobia	fear of falling from high places
batophobia	fear of high objects (towers, mountains)
carophobia	fear of insects
coprophobia	repugnance to filth, dirt
cynophobia	fear of dogs, of getting rabies
demophobia	fear of crowds
doraphobia	fear of touching animal hair or fur
ergasiophobia	dislike of work, fear of taking responsibility
gamophobia	fear of marriage
gehrophobia	fear of crossing a bridge over water
gynephobia	fear of women
necrophobia	fear of dead bodies
nudophobia	fear of being seen unclothed
ophidiophobia	fear of harmless snakes
pantophobia	fear of the future
peccatiphobia	fear of committing social errors
pharmacophobia	fear of medicine

photophobia	fear of light
psychrophobia	fear of cold
pyrophobia	fear of fire
rhabdophobia	fear of being eaten
scopophobia	fear of being observed
scotophobia	fear of darkness
sitophobia	fear of eating
thalassaphobia	fear of sea voyage
toxicophobia	fear of being poisoned
zoophobia	fear of animals in general

Quite a list! And it is incomplete. Another phobia that could be added is agoraphobia, the subject of several recent syndicated newspaper articles. Agoraphobia is literally the fear (*phobos*-phobia) of the marketplace (*agora*)—or the fear of going out where people are.

The *Chicago Tribune* printed the desperate plea of a Pontiac, Michigan, man who was seeking help for a sister who was agoraphobic. "My sister," said the man, "has suffered for years a fear of going outside, so much that she seldom ventures out of the house." He was asking a medical doctor who writes regularly for the *Tribune* specifically about drug therapy.

The physician had been asked such questions before. Agoraphobia, he said, causes people to suffer "spontaneous attacks of pain when out in public . . . so severe and so unpredictable that the patient eventually avoids all social situations."[2] He didn't offer much help, besides describing two drugs, warning that heavy doses causing dangerous side effects would be required to produce the desired result.

If I could speak with this woman, I know what I would do. I would go to her, put my arm around her, and walk with her to the front door. Then I would take her outside and show her that she has nothing to fear in the out-of-doors. I would repeat to her some of the "fear nots" from the Bible. I would assure her that "God hath not given us the spirit of fear; but of power, and of love, and of a sound mind" (2 Tim. 1:7).

Where Did Fear Originate?

The Bible tells us that man as created by God was completely good, perfect. God gave man authority and dominion over the earth, over every creature in the heavens, on the earth, and in the seas. There is no hint of fear in the creation account. Adam named all the beasts (Gen. 2:19,20)—including the lion, tiger, and bear—and nothing suggests that he harbored fear of any of them.

But in the third chapter of Genesis, immediately after Adam and Eve sinned, fear reared its ugly head. God came seeking man, asking him, "Where are you?" And Adam said, ". . . I heard thy voice in the garden, and *I was afraid,* because I was naked; and I hid myself" (Gen. 3:10, italics mine).

Fear has been man's constant companion since that day when sin entered Paradise, and Adam and Eve were forced to flee the Garden. Occasionally we are told that the primitive peoples who have remained largely untouched by civilization are happy. But I have not found them so. In my travels in a hundred nations, I have had occasion many times to enter the villages of the more primitive peoples. My consistent finding is that those who do not know God are beset with fear. They revere stone and wooden idols, and they are afraid of insulting their dead ancestors. They are terribly afraid of the dark—and there is no darkness like the darkness of the jungle night. They become superstitious when disease comes, and they fear storms. But I have observed that when they embrace the gospel, fear leaves them. With God's help, they overcome their primitive terrors.

77

Fear Not!

Newborn infants seem to have but two fears—almost without exception, they will cry at sudden, loud noises and at the threat of being dropped. All other fears are learned. Little children have to be warned to fear dogs; otherwise they will approach any dog, large or small, and seek to pet it. They will do this with any animal or bird that does not flee at their approach. They do not fear fire or heights, either. Instruction reinforced by personal experience teaches a child to fear.

While we should respect that which can do us harm, we should not be victims of fear. Turning to our Bibles, we find that God continually bids us not to be afraid. At least three-hundred-sixty-five times in the Bible we are told, "Fear not." That's a directive for each day of the year.

In the first book of the Bible, the Lord tells Abraham, ". . . Fear not, Abram: I am thy shield, and thy exceeding great reward" (Gen. 15:1). And in the last book, Jesus Christ says, "Fear none of those things which thou shalt suffer . . ." (Rev. 2:10).

God said to the judges of Israel, ". . . Ye shall not be afraid of the face of man . . ." (Deut. 1:17).

He told Joshua, the captain of the young nation of Israel, to tell his men, ". . . Fear not, nor be dismayed, be strong and of good courage . . ." (Josh. 10:25). Joshua had just assumed the reins of the nation; Moses was dead, and the people of Israel were in enemy territory. There were giants in the land and walled cities—but God, through Joshua, said, "Fear not."

That beautiful man of God, David, declared: "God is our refuge and strength, a very present help in trouble. Therefore will not we fear, though the earth be removed, and though the mountains be carried into the midst of the sea" (Ps. 46:1,2).

Isaiah echoed it. ". . . I will trust, and not be afraid: for the

Lord JEHOVAH is my strength and my song . . ." (Isa. 12:2).

Daniel quaked in fear when God showed him a vision, but an angel touched and reassured him. ". . . O man greatly beloved fear not: peace be unto thee, be strong, yea, be strong . . ." (Dan. 10:19).

To shepherds on the hillside, an angel declared, ". . . Fear not: for, behold, I bring you good tidings of great joy, which shall be to all people" (Luke 2:10).

All through his life, Jesus bid fear to flee. On the waters of Galilee, when meeting people in distress—wherever He went—he said, "Fear not, fear not." Upon meeting the disciples after His death, after three days of hopeless despair, the risen Christ said, "Fear not."

Paul told his young disciple, Timothy, "For God hath not given us the spirit of fear; but of power, and of love, and of a sound mind" (2 Tim. 1:7).

John wrote it so well: "There is no fear in love; but perfect love casteth out fear: because fear hath torment. He that feareth is not made perfect in love" (1 John 4:18).

Turn the Light on Your Fears

How can we overcome our fears? Faith shows the way. Talking about our fears and understanding that they are groundless does not always make them go away. Most little children do not like to go outside at night by themselves, because they fear the darkness. You can explain to a child that nothing is going to "get" him if he goes outside to close the garage door after dark, but that doesn't help him. You can tell a four-year-old to go up to her room on the darkened second floor, but she will be afraid unless you go with her or, at least, turn on the lights.

The Polish novelist Jerzy Kosinski once said on an interview program that he has nightmares when he visits cities of Europe where uniformed military and policemen are highly visible.

"I dream I am back in Eastern Europe," he said. "The police are after me, and I cannot get away. It is quite frightening. Not until I wake up, turn on the light, and see where I am does the fear go away."

Kosinski does what a child would do; he turns on the light. He really has nothing to fear, since dreams can hurt no one. By turning on the light, he returns to reality. This is a basic principle: Much of what we fear will never bother us again if we see it for what it is. God is light, and by turning to God's Word, we can see that nothing should terrorize or paralyze us. By continuing to absorb biblical truth, through daily reading and study, we will walk in the light as He is in the light; and in that blessed environment, fear cannot get to us.

If you are bothered by fears, I suggest you practice the daily reading of the Bible. Let your trust grow as you study the Gospels and read how Jesus delivered people from demons, from illness, from sin. Read of these deliverances and claim victory over your own fears. God can do it again. Continue to read other Christian books and the Bible, and let your faith grow. Practice Christian love; you will discover that "love casteth out fear" (1 John 4:18).

Pray Often

No one needs to be told to pray when he is afraid. For some people, indeed, that is the *only* time they pray. But there's sufficient evidence that God hears foxhole prayers, too. We are immediately comforted when we pray, because in prayer we realize that we are not alone.

Tell your heavenly Father you are afraid. I know a young man who worked in the headquarters of a church denomination, where it was the custom to meet once a week for prayer and worship. He was chosen to give a devotional talk, and, although he had spoken before groups dozens of times, this particular assignment paralyzed him. He didn't know what he was going to say, and he was afraid of losing his colleagues' respect. Driving to work, he felt panicky, but then he began blurting out his fears to God. "I don't know what I am going to say, God," he pleaded. "I don't even want to do this." Before long, however, his mind was filled with conversation that led him, surprisingly, to the conviction that he *did* have something to say after all. His fears subsided.

> Oh, what peace we often forfeit,
> Oh, what needless pain we bear,
> All because we do not carry,
> Everything to God in prayer![3]

Confess Your Freedom From Fear

For most of my life I have been gloriously free of fear. Once, while on my first preaching trip around the world, I was forced to walk a trail in China for three hours with a gun to my head. But I was not afraid; I did not collapse in fear, because the peace of God filled my heart. God told me that I would live, so I turned around and laughed in the faces of the soldiers.

On that same trip, Howard Carter and I entered forbidden Tibet, traveling on muleback. For three months we lived in that country, often sleeping in the dark pagan temples with their evil-looking idols. I do not remember being afraid. On another occasion, a small plane in which I was flying in Mexico went down and turned over. I was shaken up, but not hurt. Had I listened to some of the people who saw what had happened, I would never have flown again. But why should I limit myself? I took the next plane out and have flown hundreds of thousands of miles since then.

If the devil tells me not to do something, that's the very thing I will do. If he tells me that a door is shut, I will kick the door down. We must not be afraid of the devil. The Bible tells us, ". . . Resist the devil, and he will flee from you" (James 4:7). Testify daily that you are free, saying: "I am free from all my fears. I am not afraid."

[1]Paul Tournier, *Reflections* (New York: Harper & Row, 1974), pp. 19–20.

[2]G. Timothy Johnson, "How to Keep Well," *Chicago Tribune* (Jan., 1979).

[3]Joseph Scriven, "What a Friend We Have in Jesus."

6

Out of the Depths of Depression

I waited patiently for the Lord; and he inclined unto me, and heard
  my cry.
He brought me up also out of an horrible pit, out of the miry clay,
And set my feet upon a rock, and established my goings.
And he hath put a new song in my mouth, even praise unto our God:
many shall see it, and fear, and shall trust in the Lord (Ps. 40:1–3).

Those who are depressed wallow in the "d's" of depression—discouragement, despair, disappointment, despondency, dejection, defeat, and disgust.

The person sinking into a deepening depression begins to be preoccupied with feelings of failure, sinfulness, worthlessness, and despair. He cannot be reasoned with or told to cheer up, for his woe is an internal event that does not correspond to reality as others see it. Overcome with his personal hopelessness, the depressive cuts off communication with the outside world, abandons active attempts to help himself, and usually begins to contemplate ending it all by suicide. The depressive may not hallucinate, but he may descend to such a stuporous level of mental and physical inactivity that he may be bed-ridden and require force-feeding.[1]

Depression reveals itself in a person's countenance. He

looks depressed. His face is sad, his shoulders droop as if carrying the burdens of the world, and his entire appearance may become unkempt. Mentally reliving the past causes the depressive to cringe with guilt, shame, self-hatred, self-pity, and anger. He feels unloved and alone, unworthy of attention even if anyone did care. Hopelessness feeds on pessimism, so no solution is quite sufficient for the depressive's particular situation. As if pulled into some giant vacuum, his entire personality is sucked inward to focus on introspection and self-obsession. Like Alice in Wonderland, the depressive lives in a world where self is bigger than life.

As depression progresses, biochemical changes may take place in the body, causing changes in appetite, sleep, weight patterns, and bodily functions. Often when a depressive seeks medical help for these physical ailments, the physician treats only the symptoms, without dealing with the source of the problem.

What Causes It?

What causes depression?

The authors of *Happiness Is a Choice* list three causes: (1) Lack of self-worth. (2) Lack of intimacy with others—loneliness. (3) Lack of intimacy with God.[2]

A lack of self-worth may result from damage to one's self-image through ridicule, rejection, failure, disappointment, or defeat. False guilt also can contribute to poor self-esteem. Persons overly self-critical tend to blame *themselves* for their defeats.

A lack of intimacy with others may develop through no fault of our own but through some personal loss—death, divorce, a job, a move, or a loss of personal freedom. Because we have not caused this loss ourselves, we often develop anger toward those who did. If we cannot or will not express this anger to those who are responsible, we turn the anger inward, becoming angry with ourselves.

Nevertheless, our alienation from others, our loneliness, may be our own doing. Because of emotional pain, we may withdraw from life, avoiding occasions of contact with people, sometimes retreating instead to the company of cats and dogs.

Depression usually develops when our relationship with God is not what it should be. A thing or a person may come between us and God. Then, when a traumatic experience comes our way—illness, disappointment, or loss of a loved one—we have cut ourselves off from our only source of spiritual strength.

If we are demoralized, physically and mentally over-extended, and spiritually dry, we do not have the will power necessary to keep from slipping into the abyss of depression. We must build up our other resources before our wills can be revived. We can then take steps to rise out of depression.

We need the Lord in every aspect of our lives—to forgive our sin, to give us victory over Satan, to guide us down life's path, and to give us wisdom for decisions, comfort in sorrow, and strength to continue when the way is rough. When we short-circuit our intimacy with Him, for whatever reason, we become vulnerable to depression.

We *cannot* handle true guilt on our own. We *cannot* handle Satan's attacks on our own. We *cannot* live the Christian life through our own efforts. Only when the Lord is our whole life, does the whole of our life fall into place.

"Learned" Depression

Depression beyond our control can be caused by faulty metabolism, thyroid problems, hypoglycemia, and shifts to the next stage of growth, as in puberty. Beyond this, however, depression is not inherited, but it can be learned. A child learns to deal with anger, frustrations, and problems by observing how his parents deal with them. If the parent's anger is expressed through a savage temper, the child learns to handle his anger the same way.

Depression, sometimes called "the common cold of psychopathology," is not only a modern malady. The Bible provides case histories of many who were depressed, including King Ahab, one of Israel's monarchs during the nation's decline in the eighth century B.C.

Israel was faltering before the threats of King Ben-hadad of Syria to the north and staggering from years of godless rule by Ahab's predecessors in Samaria. All of the king's seers were yellow-bellied "yes men" who waited to see what the king wanted before uttering their prophetic words. Another irritation to Ahab was Elijah, the man of God, who had stopped rain from falling in Israel for three-and-a-half years and who had humiliated the king's seers by calling down fire from heaven.

But King Ahab's greatest source of depression confronted him daily at home; he had Jezebel for a wife. She was probably one of the most conniving, evil females who had ever walked the face of the earth.

One day Ahab came home to his palace, depressed. He ". . . came into his house heavy and displeased because of the word which Naboth the Jezreelite had spoken to him. . . . And he laid him down upon his bed, and turned away his face, and would eat no bread" (1 Kings 21:4).

In the city of Samaria, humble Naboth, the farmer, owned choice property adjacent to the palace of King Ahab and Queen Jezebel. Ahab coveted Naboth's vineyard. He had made Naboth an offer, but Naboth wasn't interested. In Israel, a man did not sell his family property; it was his inheritance and was to be passed on to his sons. So, Ahab, sullen and sad, went home and went to bed.

He might have remained depressed for a long time had it

not been for Jezebel. Coming in and seeing the king with his face turned to the wall, she asked: "Why is your spirit so sad, that you eat no bread?" Upon hearing the pouting Ahab, she immediately had Naboth killed and took possession of the vineyard. Such drastic action is not recommended in dealing with depression!

God's Servants Get Depressed

Even a man of God like Elijah became so depressed that he wished to die. In 1 Kings 18 the story is told of his victorious confrontation with Ahab's chosen false prophets on Mount Carmel and his subsequent outdistancing of Ahab's chariot all the way back to the capital city, Samaria. The experience on Mount Carmel was exhilarating; but Elijah had to come back to everyday existence. Jezebel was after his head. He left the city and traveled night and day into the desert. "When we are tired and discouraged, unexpected pressure or disappointment can knock the bottom out of life."[3]

Elijah was convinced he was the only faithful believer left in Israel. He would eat nothing, preferring to die. Fear, fatigue, and failure (1 Kings 19:10) made him wish for death. As with Elijah, "depression often arises from unfulfilled hopes and ruined expectations. He had expected [the pressures] to all be over. Instead there was tremendous pressure because of Jezebel's death threat."[4]

An angel found him in a cave and fed him. The food and rest and the assurance that God still had work for him to do brought him out of depression. "Nowhere in this account did God condemn or scold Elijah. God wanted to restore and rebuild him to enable him to again carry on the work God had for him."[5]

For the deeply depressed, knowing the symptoms and causes of depression is not enough. They may ask, "So what?" or "Now what do I do?" That is exactly what Jesus is waiting to hear. He loves us and cares what is happening to us. "Cast . . . all your care upon him; for he careth for you (1 Pet. 5:7). The Lord desires and is able to help us out of our depression.

A Christian mother of four children, after learning that her physical problems were caused by depression, sought the Lord's deliverance.

Her first step was prayer. She opened her soul and poured out her heart to the Lord. "Forgive me, Father, for allowing myself to get into this condition. I realize that not all that has happened is my own doing, so forgive those who have contributed to my depression. Thank You for allowing all this to happen to me so that in Your working I can observe how much You *do* love me and how wonderful and great a God You are."

Her first need was to realize completely that Jesus loved her. She knew John 3:16. In fact, she knew a lot of facts about the Bible. But now the Lord was going to allow her to experience the Living Word of God. All she prayed was, "Lord, I know this is terrible to say after all You have done for me on the cross, but would You show me that You love *me?*

She was an avid reader, so the Lord used the printed page—books and articles—to speak to her. One of the books that made a great impact was *Love Is Now* by Peter Gillquist. Her greatest excitement and amazement, though, came from reading the Bible. It was as if the Lord Himself were sitting there, speaking to her those words she so desperately wanted to hear.

She began to understand that no matter what kind of Christian she was, no matter what she did or did not do for the Lord, His love for her was not affected. His love was unconditional.

Another area in which she desperately needed the Lord's touch was her self-image. In her Christian upbringing, she had been taught that to think of herself in any way but as the "lowest of the lowly" was prideful. Pride is one of the seven sins God hates (Prov. 6:16,17), and she thought she had to put herself down to avoid this sin.

In a rather amazing way the Lord introduced her to a series of taped sermons on biblical self-image. She began to realize that God would not create anything, including herself, that was shoddy. She found that she could appropriate all that Christ is into her life by allowing Him to dwell freely in her heart.

A missionary to Thailand had a nervous breakdown because, as he says, "I invented an impossible God." He knew that He had been saved by grace and that salvation is a gift that cannot be earned. Yet, he began to feel that

life was one long, deadly grind of trying to be perfect to earn the daily pleasure of a God who simply could not be pleased. His demands were so high and his opinion of me so low, that there was no way I could really live under anything but his frown. I could work and work and never succeed in maintaining a decent relationship with him. In fact I found I had to keep scrubbing myself in God's bathtub.[6]

His long journey to healing and rediscovery included guidance by a psychiatrist. "No 'oughts.' No pat solutions. No criticisms of my Christian faith. And above all no condemnation."[7] He was helped to see himself—"my unreasonable self-expectations, my perfectionism, my bondage to other people's opinions, my doormat mentality, my self-hatred."[8]

His pastor's advice proved invaluable: "I want you to promise that you won't read the Bible or pray again until you really want to. This "freed him from inflaming the old wound of his spiritual inadequacies" and "called him beyond dutiful religion."[9]

Another step of his journey was "refusing to let myself be pushed around by my own diseased self-expectations, or by what I imagined other people expected, or even by what my diseased conscience told me God expected.''[10]

Then he learned to "accept God's acceptance. This meant that I not only had to believe that God accepted me just as I was, but I had to accept myself in the same way.''[11]

He also "had to learn to affirm my sonship; to learn to rejoice in what God had made when he created me.''[12]

The difficult part was that he "had to learn to put grace into my relationships. I had to learn the kind of interpersonal acceptance, openness and mutual giving that only grace could bring about.''[13]

How to Recover

The first step to recovery from depression is to admit you are depressed. Do not be afraid of it or ashamed to admit it. Face the issue. Until you are ready to do that, you cannot rid yourself of depression. You have to be willing to say, ''I am depressed and know it, and I want to be free by the power of God.''

I am not asking you to feel anything as yet. If you will admit being depressed, the next step is to say *by faith,* ''As a Christian I am capable of doing something about depression.'' You have dominion, strength, and power, because God has placed these within you. When you recognize what God has placed in you as a Christian, you can say to depression, ''Go!''

You do not need to doubt. Listen to what Jesus said: ''I am the vine, ye are the branches: . . . without me ye can do nothing'' (John 15:5). ''. . . In the world ye shall have tribulation: but be of good cheer; I have overcome the world'' (John 16:33). ''. . . Greater is he that is in you, than he that is in the world'' (1 John 4:4). And Paul: ''Thanks be unto God, which always causeth us to triumph in Christ . . .'' (2 Cor. 2:14). ''I

can do all things through Christ which strengtheneth me"
(Phil. 4:13).

Take Command of Your Emotions

We must be determined: "Today will be a good day. I am
going to love somebody else today." Our wills must be
brought under divine control. Memorize the words of the
psalmist: "This is the day which the Lord hath made; we *will*
rejoice and be glad in it" (Ps. 118:24, italics added). Repeat
this daily, several times a day, until you are saying it with
conviction.

Like mercury in a thermometer, our emotions rise and fall
according to our moods. Two people may have identical
experiences, and while one is saddened, the other may actually be glad. While I was preparing to speak on this subject for
one of my *Today With Lester Sumrall* TV programs, a friend
stopped in to say that his house had burned down two weeks
earlier. Then he said, "God meant it for good. I have never
had so many good things happen as have happened in the last
two weeks." He had discovered friends he never thought he
had.

For two years I lived in England, working with Smith
Wigglesworth, the Full Gospel preacher of international re-
nown. I can never remember finding him low in spirit. One
day I asked him, "Mr. Wigglesworth, I have never known
you to be depressed. Not even once have I seen you sad or
down. How do you do it?"

"Young man," he said, "when I wake up in the morning, I
don't ask Smith Wigglesworth how he feels. I *tell* him how he
is going to feel." And that was that.

There are many other ways to overcome depression. If you
are one who sleeps a lot to escape the pain of facing the
source of your depression, plan to ease yourself into the

mainstream. One housewife made herself get up early three mornings a week, regardless of how she felt. A depressed divorceé got a part-time job just so she would have to get up four mornings a week.

Draw up a plan of action that will work for you. Develop new interests and activities. Drive home a different way. Invite one special person to lunch—someone you trust, someone you admire. Sign up for an evening class. Do volunteer work. Purchase indoor plants or start a garden. Attend fellowship groups at church. Do something nice for someone each week—send a card, make a phone call, give a gift, share a good book.

Learn to respond rather than react. Learn to laugh. Develop a friendship with one special person. Don't do things that make you feel guilty. Get rid of grudges daily, and leave "getting even" to the Lord. He promised to take care of it (Rom. 12:17–19).

Take full responsibility for your actions. Establish a daily routine, but do not feel guilty if you occasionally break with it. Make a list of all the things you would really like to do, then do one each week. Listen to a record of "praise songs."

Take an interest in your person again. Style your hair in a way becoming to you. Check your wardrobe—give anything away that does not make you feel good about yourself. As you can afford it, buy yourself one complete new outfit. Do what you need to do to bring your weight under control. If you need to lose weight, begin the battle. If you need to gain weight, do what is necessary.

According to Lois Timnick of the *Los Angeles Times*, "Running is the newest treatment for depression." In an experiment at the University of Wisconsin, patients treated with "running therapy" were compared to those treated with conventional psychotherapy. It was found that "running reduced symptoms of depression." Follow-up through one year shows that most patients who were treated with running have become regular runners and remain symptom free.[14]

A big plus in overcoming depression is to realize that there *is hope*. There is hope for every person; there is hope for you. So many others are asking the question David asked in Psalm 43:5: "Why art thou cast down, O my soul? and why art thou disquieted within me?" In that same verse, he supplied the answer, "Hope in God; for I shall yet praise him, who is the health of my countenance, and my God."

Nothing is impossible with the Lord nor too hard for Him (Luke 1:37; Jer. 32:17).

[1]*Psychology Today, An Introduction*, 2nd ed. (Del Mar, Calif.: CMR Books, 1970), pp. 515–16.

[2]Frank B. Minirth, M.D., and Paul D. Meier, M.D., *Happiness is a Choice* (Grand Rapids, Mich.: Baker, 1978), p. 54.

[3]James F. Conway, "God's Rx for Depression," *Moody Monthly* (Jan. 1978), pp. 86–89.

[4]*Ibid.*

[5]*Ibid.*

[6]Joseph Cooke, "I Invented an Impossible God," *Eternity* (May, 1978), pp. 37–39.

[7]*Ibid.*

[8]*Ibid.*

[9]*Ibid.*

[10]*Ibid.*

[11]*Ibid.*

[12]*Ibid.*

[13]*Ibid.*

[14]Lois Timnick, "Depressed? Running Heralded as Newest Treatment," from *The Los Angeles Times*, published in *The Courier-News*, Bridgewater, N.J. (June 5, 1978).

7

A More Confident You

I can do all things through Christ which strengtheneth me (Phil. 4:13).

Surgeon Maxwell Maltz, the author of *Psycho-Cybernetics,* found that plastic surgery did wonders for most people on whom he operated. More often than not, persons with humped noses or "taxi-door ears" or scarred faces became happy, outgoing human beings following surgery, he learned.

But not all of his patients experienced this about-face in attitude. This led him to conclude that changing a person's looks is not the real key to changing his personality.

Maltz came to believe that self-image—how we feel about ourselves, how we perceive ourselves in *our* world—is the determining factor. He observed that those who did nothing about some freakish feature of their anatomies but who had positive, expanding self-images were the people who usually had no lack of self-confidence. "The development of an adequate, realistic self-image seems to imbue the individual with new capabilities, new talents and literally turns failure into success," wrote Dr. Maltz.[1]

This "adequate, realistic self-image" is what I equate with

self-confidence. To be without self-confidence is to be crippled, hampered in the essential actions of our lives, severely handicapped in reaching those goals we have set for ourselves. The world has been robbed of true genius by lack of self-confidence. Many people with whom I counsel confess to a fear of not being able to get the job they want, not being able to develop satisfying relationships with other people, not being able to succeed in things that mean very much to them. They *distrust* themselves. They are *diffident,* timid, too quiet to speak up, and too backward to come forward. They are easily *discouraged;* if they are told they cannot do a thing, they give up. They *despair* of ever seeing a change. They are *discontent,* but not enough to fight back and prove to others and themselves that they can succeed. They expect *disappointment;* they are often *depressed.*

What Are the Causes of Self-Doubt?

It would be easy, perhaps, if all our self-doubts could be traced to external factors. If crooked teeth or ugly cavities mar a smile, a dentist can take care of that. If a facial feature is undesirable, plastic surgery can come to the rescue. If clothes are unattractive, a new wardrobe remedies the problem. To a degree, self-help seminars and courses can instill feelings of poise, self-reliance, and self-esteem. Besides the fact that most of these remedies cost money and thus are out of the reach of many people, there are many external factors that we cannot so easily change.

To come under heavy criticism when young can shatter a person's self-confidence. I think of a young man who seemed never to measure up to his father's expectations. He remembers being constantly criticized for the way he cut the lawn or kept his room. When he was old enough to have a driver's license, his dad took him to a parking lot to practice. After only a few minutes behind the wheel, the youth was told that he was too uncoordinated to learn to drive. It was not until he was a sophomore in college that he persuaded older boys to give him lessons and finally got his license. When this young man went out for track at the university, he had no confidence that he could excel. As a result his athletic accomplishments were mediocre. Now a grown man, he is still dogged by self-doubt.

Parents often do not realize that by calling their children demeaning names such as "dummy" and "stupid," they are planting seeds of self-doubt—and even self-hate—in their children's minds. We tend to become that which we think we are. "For as he thinketh in his heart, so is he . . ." (Prov. 23:7).

To be given too great responsibility too soon can also create self-doubt. A person who is called on to assume heavy responsibilities too early in life cannot help making major mistakes. A teenage girl who has to become "mother" to her younger brothers and sisters after her mother dies may feel grave doubts about ever having children of her own. A young man placed in a managerial role prematurely can make such disastrous mistakes and feel that he is such a failure that he dares not venture into a responsibile position again.

Such persons must realize that there is purpose even in these painful experiences. The two mentioned above probably had little or no choice in assuming responsibilities before they were ready; they have no reason to blame themselves. I would encourage such persons to believe in themselves. What they have learned in unfortunate circumstances can be put to good use in future responsibilities.

Not being prepared is another cause of self-doubt. Dr. Maltz points out that it does little good to try to talk ourselves into self-confidence. "You cannot merely imagine a new self-image unless you feel that it is based upon truth," he says.[2] If you are not prepared for a final exam, no amount of talk will convince yourself otherwise. If you are not ready to sell a product, or make a speech, or give a report to your employer, you cannot help feeling inadequate and timid.

War hero Eddie Rickenbacker was the leading American ace in World War I, claiming twenty-two enemy planes and two balloons. He was always prepared for combat. It seems that some of his fellow pilots had had close shaves with the enemy when their machine guns jammed during combat. When this happened to Rickenbacker, he adopted a new habit. At night, while his buddies were in bed, he went out to his plane on the flight line and inspected his ammunition, seeing that every bullet would insert easily into the machine. The next day he flew with confidence.

We cannot blame anyone else for our failure to be prepared. As responsible, maturing men and women, we can take steps to be prepared the next time an opportunity presents itself. This will give us confidence for our present duties and instill a sense of readiness for what may be ahead of us.

Sometimes, *a natural impediment or handicap* will make a person stay in the background, afraid to enter the mainstream of life. Lisping speech, a facial blemish, a crippled limb—these may stand in our way. The stories of people who have overcome these handicaps are so numerous that we cannot be discouraged. It would surprise us to know how many pastors and well-known speakers once were plagued with stuttering speech.

Moses may not have stuttered, but when God called upon him to lead the nation of Israel out of Egypt he offered many excuses. One of them was: ". . . I am not eloquent, neither heretofore, nor since thou hast spoken unto thy servant: but I am slow of speech, and of a slow tongue" (Exod. 4:10). Notice that he is not *only* pleading a lack of ability to speak but also a lack of experience, a natural obstacle in achieving self-confidence. God replied to Moses, ". . . Who hath made man's mouth? or who maketh the dumb, or deaf, or the seeing, or the blind? have not I the Lord? Now therefore go, and I will be with thy mouth, and teach thee what thou shalt say" (vv. 11,12). *The New Bible Commentary: Revised* says, "Moses is made aware that he is pleading impotence before the Omnipotent who bestows and increases faculties and gifts as He wills, and he is promised that he will learn to speak by speaking what he is taught by God."[3]

A loss of self-respect through sin will erode your confidence. Like termites eating steadily away at the foundation of a home, the secret sins in a man's life may go unnoticed for a while. Unless a man deals with such sins, his personality will lose its "keen edge." An alcoholic who fails to admit his problem and seek help cannot withstand the fierce competition of business. A person who indulges his lustful imagination soon learns not to respect himself. He allows more and more of the world and the devil to occupy a place in his bodily temple, and this takes away from the force of his personality.

There is a close relationship between self-confidence and self-respect; lack of self-confidence can be a spiritual problem.

Increase Your Self-Confidence

The new birth brings with it renewed potential for self-esteem and, thus, self-confidence. In recent years the term "born again" has almost lost its meaning. Being born again is what happens when a person puts his faith in God through His Son Jesus Christ. He is converted, saved, delivered from judgment and the consequences of his sin because he has accepted God's gracious love through Jesus.

Before I was converted at age seventeen, I lied every time I opened my mouth, it seemed. I told a lie when the truth fit best, and immediately I met my own lies coming back at me. But when I gave my life to Christ it became easy for me to tell

99

the truth. I was changed on the inside. I suddenly knew I could tell the truth, and that brought me self-confidence.

"The unhappy, failure-type personality cannot develop a new self-image by pure will power," says Dr. Maltz, "or by arbitrarily deciding to. . . . Experience has shown that when a person does change his self-image he has the feeling that for one reason or another, he 'sees' or realizes the truth about himself."[4] This is why conversion and the forgiveness of sins are so essential to a healthy self-confidence. A Christian has every reason to be self-confident. He has been forgiven all his sins. He is a child of God (1 John 3:2). God has accepted him into His family, and he is a child of the King! These are not mere words, for we know that in the beginning God made us in His own image (Gen. 1:27). Through original sin—the sin of Adam and Eve—all have fallen from that high place, but now in Christ we are restored to be joint-heirs with Christ (Rom. 8:17); we are ". . . a chosen generation, a royal priesthood, an holy nation . . ." (1 Pet. 2:9).

While a right relationship with God is a prerequisite for a healthy self-image, being a Christian does not automatically mean that we will be self-confident. We must still learn to give up the lifelong habits of downgrading ourselves, of being lazy, of thinking that we have no great worth. Dr. Maltz requires that those who follow his psycho-cybernetics practice "creative imagination" for at least three weeks before expecting to see a change in their self-images. He reasons that we need time to implant such a radical new way of living and thinking.

I agree. Having entered into a new relationship with God, we need to experience daily the affirming presence of God. We may not have been loved or praised or accepted for ourselves by our parents or friends. But God loves us as we are and forgives us. He has high aspirations for us. We are His ". . . workmanship, created in Christ Jesus unto good works . . ." (Eph. 2:10). Daily Scripture reading and regular worship will begin to implant the right ideas in our minds.

There is a further spiritual step necessary—*"receiving the Holy Spirit."* We receive Him at the time we place our faith in Jesus Christ, but we need to make a full commitment of our lives to God and thus know the filling of the Spirit. Jesus told the early disciples, "Ye shall receive power, after that the Holy Ghost is come upon you . . ." (Acts 1:8). He could just as easily have said, "You shall receive confidence." The Spirit gives power for every task in life—for witnessing, for loving, for helping others, for doing our jobs. Some churches teach that we ought to ask God to baptize us with His Spirit, while others teach that we commit ourselves fully to God through Christ and receive His power. It does not matter so much how we describe the experience. What is essential is that we surrender our lives completely and then actively trust Him to live His power-filled life through us. The Scripture says, "Ye are of God, little children, and have overcome them: because greater is he that is in you, than he [Satan] that is in the world" (1 John 4:4).

The changes we might expect to see in our lives are manifest in the apostle Peter. Before he received the Spirit, he could not testify before a little maiden who asked him if he was one of Jesus' followers. But after the Spirit filled him, Peter had no fear. He publicly preached in Jerusalem only weeks after Jesus was crucified. He had a confidence born of the Holy Spirit.

A very practical step toward increasing self-confidence is simply to *try hard.* This is what Eddie Rickenbacker did, and it is what everyone can do.

After living overseas and doing missionary work for a number of years, I returned to the States and enrolled for some classes at the University of Chicago. Immediately I found that the other students were far ahead of me. I had not

101

even gone to college before. It was not unusual for me to feel that the class material was over my head. But so great was my desire to learn that when a particular class period ended I asked the instructor where that same subject was being taught again. He looked at his schedule and gave me the name of the building and the hour. I took my notes to that second class period and tried to learn what I had not been able to grasp in the first session. By the end of the semester I had the only A in class. I found that I could learn as well as the other men in the class; the extra work compensated for my having been away from school a number of years.

To try, and try again, creates a growing sense of confidence. When you know that you know, then you really *know*. Self-confidence grows out of competence.

A young man entered the Air Force and chose flying school. He had never flown in his life, but he thought that if he could qualify he would enjoy flying more than anything else in the Air Force. In Florida, his class began learning the basics in the PA-18 Super Piper. This young man was progressing well, but he could not do the one thing that is essential to flying—*land the airplane*. He had a few problems with flying, too, but he was plagued primarily by a total lack of confidence in his ability to land the little plane. After twelve hours with one instructor and no solo flight, he was switched to another instructor. Then, just before he washed out of the flying program, he soloed. But he went on leave for two weeks immediately after, and when he returned, he was afraid he would not be able to fly. Taxiing out for that next flight, he confessed his fears to his instructor, who asked him, "You didn't forget how to swim and have to learn all over again from one summer to the next, did you?"

"No," the young pilot answered, getting the point. His flight was a success that day, and he went on to graduate months later, flying heavy jet aircraft. It took work, continued effort, practice, and more work, but with each session

102

he became more confident. That is how we gain self-confidence.

Finally, we can increase our self-confidence by simply *dressing to look our best.* The right clothes help to make us feel better about ourselves. Properly attired, we can forget about our appearance and enjoy being with others. We can enter into whatever we do without fearing that people are looking at us and our clothing. Our looks often determine whether we are accepted by others, so it is important to look well-groomed and to dress right for each occasion.

A neat coat and tie, a shine on the shoes, well-combed hair, clean and evenly-trimmed fingernails—these are part of our preparedness. Looking nice and smelling clean free us to be confident in any occasion.

A young woman working for a missionary organization received only a small salary. She could have gotten by on older clothing that would have made her self-conscious about her appearance, but instead she dressed attractively. In that way, "I can continue to carry on my work of counseling other young women with confidence—and forget about myself," she said.

Self-confidence is not pride or bigotry. Self-confidence is not a cosmetic to cover our faces. It has its roots deep in our spirits. It is the outflowing of an internal strength. God can give you enough confidence to be the man or woman or young person He intended you to be.

When I was fifty, a minister said to me, "Sumrall, you're fifty, and you're finished."

I could hardly believe my ears. I had devoted thirty years to missionary work and was just beginning a new ministry in Indiana. If there was anything I needed, it was confidence.

My answer was, "I'm glad you are not God, for if you were God, I might believe you. But seeing that you're not God, I don't believe you at all."

Then when I was alone with the Lord, I asked, "Am I

finished?'' He said to me, ''Sumrall, you may be fifty, but you're not finished. Get going.'' And I have been going ever since.

God is not through with us. Just as He will not allow any temptation that is too great to come our way, He also will give us the confidence and the grace for every task and responsibility that He gives us.

[1]Maxwell Maltz, M.D., *Psycho-Cybernetics* (New York: Pocket Books, Prentice-Hall, 1960), p. *ix*.

[2]*Ibid.* p. 27.

[3]D. Guthrie, J.A. Motyer, *et al. The New Bible Commentary: Revised* (Grand Rapids, Mich.: Wm. B. Eerdmans, 1970), p. 124.

[4]Maltz, *Psycho-Cybernetics,* p. 27.

8

Alone in the World

"I am like a pelican of the wilderness: I am like an owl of the desert. I watch, and am as a sparrow alone upon the house top" (Ps. 102:6, 7).

Loneliness.

Intensely, deeply, the human soul tastes of this most common of human experiences.

Right now you may feel you are all alone in the world. You are that "sparrow alone upon the housetop." Your companion has been taken from you, and you are alone. Perhaps your marriage has failed; your children are with your former wife. Or, your husband has left you for another woman, and you feel a terrible sense of rejection. You are hauntingly alone.

A thousand circumstances conspire to engulf us in loneliness. The man or woman in prison, the young mother in a city of strangers, the child in a new neighborhood or a new school, the college student away from home, the man or woman in military service—these and others are alone and lonely. Like nothing else, the steady advancement of age isolates us; our parents die, as do friends, brothers, sisters, and mates. We become feeble. No longer able to keep house, we occupy a solitary room in some home for the aged where most waking hours are spent alone in unfamiliar surroundings, separated from anyone whom we know.

Of course, we do not have to be alone to be lonely. Ask anyone who works in Manhattan. Indeed, surrounded by throngs of people—many of them walking and talking with friends, perhaps speaking a different language from ours—we can feel the pain of loneliness most keenly.

I am convinced that thousands of lonely people are in our churches Sunday after Sunday. They walk in alone, and all they receive are well-practiced smiles as they are shown to their seats. No one reaches across the pews to greet them, to learn their names, to make them feel at home. In some churches, they are not even spoken to. The former custom of inviting guests home for dinner after church is rarely practiced now; this lack of hospitality hurts the stranger all the more. In God's house he thought he could find fellowship, a warm handclasp. But all he may receive is a plastic smile and an offering envelope.

Pastors and psychologists and others who do much counseling know that a person may feel continually lonely and even alienated from himself due to experiences in his infancy or childhood. "A child who feels rejected by his parents is likely to conclude that he's not good enough to be wanted by anybody," says Dr. Craig Ellison, assistant professor of psychology at Westmont College.[1] If nothing is done to counter this *feeling* (it need not be based on truth), a person may be cut off from meaningful, satisfying relationships with others.

Children of divorced parents especially must recognize their potential feelings of low self-esteem, which can lead to increased solitude. Even more vulnerable are the children who, coming into this world unwanted by their parents, quickly see that they are unloved by the very ones who should love them the most. Whenever I meet someone who feels rejected, I want to embrace him and tell him he has great worth. We must realize that we are all made in God's image and that we have infinite potential and value in God's sight.

We say we *feel lonely* because loneliness is an attitude characterized by a gloomy outlook on life. I have observed people who say they are lonely; it sometimes seems they are getting what they deserve. That sounds harsh, but it is true. No one goes out of his way for very long to be with a gloomy person.

Loneliness is related to alienation. Its origin is in the fall of man. When Adam and Eve sinned, they hid themselves. Something had come between them, and when God came walking in the Garden and asked them what they had done, Adam turned to Eve and accused her. This pattern continues today. "Man was made for God and without God he is going to be lonely; he has a sense of alienation," says Billy Graham. "His sins, the Bible says, have separated him from God. Man thinks if he indulges in acts of pleasure he can drown his feeling of loneliness; but nothing works apart from God. The thing we are longing for is the thing we were made for."[2]

Loneliness is often associated with feelings of self-pity. "Nobody cares; nobody likes me; nobody thinks I'm wonderful," we say to ourselves, and with each word we isolate ourselves even more. Remember the childhood song, "Nobody likes me, everybody hates me, guess I'll go eat worms. . ." ?

Failure leads to loneliness. "It's lonely at the top," they say. That may be so, but it's abysmally lonely at the bottom.

The possibility of failure is always with us. We can't play it safe; we must give our all. So what if we fail? Some of our greatest growth experiences can come through failure. We must get up and try harder next time. Attitude is the key: If we think of ourselves as failures, we are already on Lonely Road. The greatest failure is not to learn from previous failures.

Loneliness Kills

A person left to himself tends to disintegrate. A man will let his hair go uncombed; he will quit shaving, and soon no one will want to be around him. Women who stay to themselves grow careless about their appearance. *Time* magazine has noted that loneliness kills. It gave examples:

The coronary death rate among widows between 25 and 34 is five times that of married women in the same age group. At all ages, the divorced are twice as likely as the married to develop lung cancer or suffer a stroke. Among divorced white males, cirrhosis of the liver is seven times more common, and tuberculosis ten times more common.[3]

Emile Cailliet, writing in *Alone at High Noon* stated that "the general consensus is that the most prevalent cause of suicide is a sense of loneliness in those who take their life."[4]

Duane Pederson, who has worked with hippies and runaways in Hollywood for many years, quotes the following letter in his book *On Lonely Street with God.*

For me, loneliness is a big killer [says Rick, a new Christian]. Ever since the fifth grade I've been in and out of schools. When I was 14 I started with marijuana and went through the line—pills, LSD, and then I started mixing speed and heroin. I was about 16 when I finally reached heroin and I began not to care about *anything.* I cared even less about *anybody,* myself included. I had a false sort of bravery and was forging checks. But after an overdose of heroin I got caught.

My parents bought me a ticket out of town to a city in another state where the job opportunities were the highest at the time. After three weeks there I hitchhiked back to find that while I'd been away—only three weeks—five of my friends had died, all of them from some form of drugs! The realization of knowing then that I was born *alone,* and I was going to die *alone,* that basically the rest of my life I would be here *alone,* hit me hard, but not hard enough!

That December I had my hands on a lot of drugs and I had given them to two of my friends and my girlfriend and they took them off in the car. Well, they were in an accident, one guy lost an eye, the other guy's scars will probably be there the rest of his life, and my *girlfriend died.*

After the funeral I really lost complete control. I didn't care about living and took as many drugs as I could get my hands on. Then I took off in a car and was in an accident myself. I woke up the next day in the county jail! Alive! I called my parents to come and bail me out, but they said, "Forget it . . . we've tried and tried to help you but there's nothing we can do, so forget it!" Then they hung up and I thought that would be the last I'd ever hear from them. I was there *alone* in the county jail!

On Christmas day I felt obligated to read the Bible there in my loneliness in the jail. I picked up a copy of *Good News for Modern Man* and started to read. I got to Matthew 10:30–36 where Jesus is telling His disciples that He has not "come to bring peace on earth but a sword" . . . "to turn some against their fathers, daughters against their mothers" and so on. Jesus went on to say, "Anyone who doesn't love Me more than these is not worthy of Me."[5]

The young rebel, Rick, went on to invite Jesus Christ into his life. Although he did not immediately see all his problems resolved, in time he was able to say, "I'm sometimes lonely now—but I'm not *alone*—and praise Jesus, *for He is always with me.*"[6]

Loneliness—An Instrument for Good

Placing so much emphasis on the adverse effects of being alone may lead to two wrong assumptions: one, that loneliness is an evil to be avoided at all costs, and two, that companionship is the basic solution.

A good deal of life is spent alone. We might imagine that if God built so much solitude into our earthly existence, He must have had a good reason for it. And that is correct. Do not misunderstand. I am not merely stating that solitude is good; that goes without saying. It is natural for humans to seek solitude on occasion. Jesus, who is our finest example, often sought solitude to pray and to prepare for events ahead of him. Before He entered upon His three-year public ministry, He went out into the desert to be alone for forty days and nights. I treasure the times when I can be alone to think, to meditate, to create. But this kind of solitude is something distinctly different from loneliness.

I believe that loneliness itself can be good, or rather, can be the vehicle of good. An illustration can be drawn from the work of Clark Moustakas, author of *Loneliness* and *Loneliness and Love*. He says that he actually began "to look into the heart of the lonely experience" when his five-year-old daughter Kerry had to have immediate surgery for a congenital heart defect.

During the two weeks while she was in the pediatric ward [my wife and I] never left Kerry's side. I had many opportunities to observe children experiencing isolation and loneliness. . . . I began to see that loneliness is neither good nor bad, but a point of intense and timeless awareness of the Self, a beginning which initiates totally new sensitivities and awareness, and which results in bringing a person deeply in touch with his own existence and in touch with others in a fundamental sense. I began to see that in the deepest experiences the human being can know—the birth of a baby, the prolonged illness or death of a loved relative, the loss of a job, the creation of a poem, a painting, a symphony, the grief of a fire, a flood, an accident—each in its own way touches upon the roots of loneliness. In each of these experiences, in the end, we must go alone. . . . It can be a new experience. It may be an experience of exquisite pain, deep fear and terror, an utterly terrible experience, yet it brings into awareness new dimensions of self, new beauty, new power for human compassion, and a reverence for the precious nature of each breathing moment.[7]

Our natural reaction upon encountering pain is to withdraw; this is the way we instinctively handle loneliness, because it is painful. But we will find that it continues to stalk our paths, and we must learn to cope with it. God uses loneliness to make us more compassionate, more aware of the preciousness of every day—more alive.

Ways We Try to Cope

Fellowship is the obvious answer to loneliness, and I heartily encourage people to enjoy the companionship of others. It is even more important today to form friendships, because we Americans live in a highly mobile society that can create tremendous emotional trauma. According to one estimate, forty million Americans move every year. Every move disrupts friendships and isolates people.

God's Book tells us that ". . . It is not good that the man should be alone" (Gen. 2:18). Our Creator said, "I will make him an help meet for him," and so woman was created. Elsewhere He said, "Two are better than one; because they have a good reward for their labor. For if they fall, the one will lift up his fellow: but woe to him that is alone when he falleth; for he hath not another to help him up" (Eccles. 4:9,10). God knew that man would be lonely without human companionship.

One way to avoid being lonely is to be friendly. We can initiate talks with others and listen to them. We may find they are as lonely as we are.

If you are a woman living alone, let another woman or a young girl move into the house with you, or move in with someone else. If you do not want to do that, then plan your life so that you have companionship now and then at mealtimes and do things with others on the weekends. Share the joys and griefs of life with someone else.

"Trust someone, and you may discover you have made a

111

close friend," say Gilbert Wrenn and Shirley Schwarzrock in *Living with Loneliness*.

Of course, when we trust another we are taking a risk, one that most of us are afraid to take because we fear that the person we trust may betray our trust. On the other hand, he may be very pleased that someone trusts him, and may trust you in turn. Anything worthwhile involves some risk, but doing nothing is riskiest of all.[8]

God has made man a social being and placed him in a family. Too many people take their families for granted until it is too late. If you have a family, or even a few relatives, treasure them highly. Thank God for them, and keep in touch with each one. Family ties become even more important as you grow older.

I was thirty-two when I married. My wife Louise was already serving in missionary work in Argentina when we met. If we had continued to live alone, pursuing some ideal of detachment from the world, we would not be nearly as happy as we are today. God has given us three sons to make our happiness complete.

When our first son Frank was born, I almost went crazy. The baby arrived ten days early, and I was two hundred miles away in a church meeting. I still remember my mother's phoning me and saying, "We have just taken Louise to the hospital. The baby is being born."

All I said was, "Whew, is that right?" Immediately I called a cab, not even waiting to tell the pastor who was my host that I was leaving town. At the airport I found a plane headed for our city, and without buying a ticket I boarded the plane.

"No, you don't," they said. "You get your ticket first."

But all I could think of was that baby. "We're having a baby, our first one. I can't get a ticket now; I'll get it later."

They told me I couldn't ride without a ticket, but I couldn't be reasoned with. "If anybody rides this plane, I am going to," I answered, and they let me stay on. Before Louise recovered in the hospital I was by her side. Then the nurse took me down the hall and showed me our baby. I was so proud that I told everyone passing by, "See that big boy? He's mine!" God was providing my wife and me with a family, and our family has been a great delight to us.

The Church

Not everyone has a family for companionship, and that is why the church is so important. As a pastor, I have seen the church help people deal with their loneliness. In the Old Testament, God commanded Israel to look after the fatherless, the widows, the strangers (Exod. 22:21,22). We must continue to do this in the church today.

I am glad to see that churches are reaching out to minister to singles, to the elderly, to widows and divorcees. Many times a lonely person will not seek our companionship himself; we must go to him, befriend him, and offer our help.

Jesus said that the church is His body and that He is the head. We are the members of His body. One may be the thumb, another an eye, another a little finger, another a rib. But we are members of one body, the church, and when we are not together in the assembly there is something missing from the body of Christ in worship, praise, and action. If you choose to stay away from the body when it is assembled, then you are cutting yourself off from the very people who need you, and whom you need.

I have seen people who were suffering from loneliness take on duties in the church and forget they were ever lonely. One of the sweetest things in the world is to teach a class of children. We so easily forget that we were little at one time. Caring for the young minds of children fills our lives and blesses others. Be happily busy in the Lord's service, and you will not be lonely.

113

Christ sent out His disciples two by two, not one by one. The first miracle He performed was at a wedding in Cana where He turned the water into wine so that all could celebrate the union of two people. By coming together in the church, or in any loving, caring group, we outwit loneliness. We share one another's joy, love, and sorrow. Everyone gets a share of the other's slice of life, and that is really living.

Cultivate the Friendship of God

Earlier, I said we might wrongly assume that companionship is the solution to loneliness. I say *wrongly*, because loneliness must be accepted for itself, for the reasons God sends it into our lives. We cannot be the kind of man or woman He wants us to be without passing through the chill of loneliness.

Abraham was called "the Friend of God" (James 2:23). A study of his life in Gensis 12–24 reveals that he was often alone. His life, which is such an example of faith, ought to encourage us.

The greatest truth for us to recognize in accepting loneliness is the truth of Immanuel, God with us! As Brother Lawrence learned, we can "practice the presence of God." With David we can find that "Yea, though I walk through the valley of the shadow of death, I will fear no evil: for thou art with me . . ." (Ps. 23:4). Jesus Himself confirms this with His parting words, "Lo, I am with you alway, even unto the end of the world" (Matt. 28:20). That is the greatest answer to loneliness.

---

[1]Craig Ellison, "Roots of Loneliness," *Christianity Today* (March 10, 1978), p. 14.

[2]Billy Graham, *Decision* (May, 1972), p. 9.

[3]"The Broken Heart: The Medical Consequences of Loneliness," *Time*, (Sept. 5, 1977), p. 45.

[4]Emile Cailliet, *Alone at High Noon* (Grand Rapids, Mich.: Zondervan, 1971), p. 59.

[5]Duane Pederson, *On Lonely Street With God* (New York: Hawthorn Books, 1973), pp. 72–73.

[6]*Ibid.*

[7]Clark Moustakas, *Loneliness* (Englewood Cliffs, N.J.: Prentice-Hall, 1961), pp. 6–7.

[8]Gilbert Wrenn and Shirley Schwarzrock, *Living With Loneliness* (Circle Pines, Minn.: American Guidance Service, Inc., 1970).

9
The Bible Is Not Silent About Deviant Sex

Sex was God's idea; he made it one of man's primary drives. Being divine in origin, sex is therefore a sacred aspect of our lives. We may be told that man gradually developed his sexual drive, that it evolved through the ages as lower forms of animal life changed into the higher forms and ultimately became man. This is not true. Sex came from God.

In this chapter we specifically discuss deviant sex. One definition of deviant sex is "that sexual activity . . . disordered by being compulsive, exclusive, destructive, accompanied by great anxiety and guilt, bizarre, inefficient or the cause of discomfort."[1]

Notice the well-chosen words within this definition. *Compulsive* means to be consumed by an overwhelming drive. Sex is good, but it is not everything. It is to be enjoyed within the bounds of a committed, lifelong relationship. On the other hand, compulsive sexual behavior breaks out of these bounds; like a fire burning out of control, it sweeps over and consumes objects in its way.

As used in the definition of deviant sex, the word *exclusive*, in my understanding, has to do with solitary sex, or masturbation, an act that is essentially selfish and exclusive. I do not think the framers of this definition intend to say that it is

117

wrong to have sex with only one partner. If that interpretation is intended, I strongly disagree.

Further, sexual conduct that is *destructive* is also deviant and therefore to be avoided. Obviously this means rape, but it can also refer to manipulative sex wherein one partner uses the other's body only for his or her physical pleasure and gratification. The New Testament teaches that the body of the husband belongs to the wife, and the wife's body belongs to the husband—but that does not allow for forced sex destructive to emotional and physical well-being.

Lastly, deviant sex is that which is "accompanied by great anxiety and guilt, [is] bizarre, inefficient or the cause of discomfort." A young married couple may read this and come to believe that their sexual activity is somehow deviating from God's original purpose if they experience anxiety or discomfort. This would be an unfortunate conclusion, since the art of love-making is not learned in a course at school or by reading books, but is mastered in experience, over some time, with communication between the couple. At first, there may be anxiety, and, for the woman, there may be discomfort.

To anyone engaging in sex outside of marriage, there will come a deep sense of anxiety accompanied by guilt, especially to those who have been taught God's law. We cannot transgress the bounds of what is right without suffering a degree of anxiety and guilt. In the sex act, we reveal ourselves more deeply to another person than through any other means. This is why God has protected sexual intercourse by restricting it to marriage. Without commitment, sex brings enormously negative psychological effects.

1 Corinthians 6:9,10 gives God's viewpoint regarding deviant sex: "Know ye not that the unrighteous shall not inherit the kingdom of God? Be not deceived: neither fornicators, nor idolaters, nor adulterers, nor effeminate, nor abusers of themselves with mankind shall inherit the kingdom of God."

It is clear what is being discussed. Deviant sex is the perversion of normal sex drives. It is homosexuality, a man making love to another man. It is lesbianism, a woman making love to a woman. It is the unspeakably sordid sexual activity that a man or woman may have with animals.

The wrong use of sex is a departure from God's intent; misuse will bring evil effects. One day, while praying, I asked God why, if a man steals or lies, people soon forget it, but if a man commits adultery we seem never to forget. God answered my question by helping me understand that a man and woman, when they come together, are the only creatures who can create a life with an immortal soul. Homosexuals cannot do that; lesbians cannot produce a child. What they do is outside the plan of God. If everyone else were as they are, soon the human race would die.

Angels cannot reproduce life. When two humans become one in sexual intercourse, they have the potential to bring into the world another person who will live eternally either in heaven or hell. Because of the profound consequence of this gift, the sex drive is protected by God's strict law. God's judgment is for anyone who breaks this law.

When I think about that, I realize that deviant sex is of the devil, not of God. The Lord created man and told the first couple to "Be fruitful and multiply . . ." (Gen. 1:22).

Homosexuality

Alfred C. Kinsey's Institute of Sex Research defines a homosexual as "anyone who has had more than six sexual experiences with a member of the same gender."[2] The Reverend Jim Conway, pastor of Twin City Bible Church, Urbana, Illinois, writing on homosexuals in *HIS* magazine says that a homosexual is one who has had "repeated experience" and who experiences "the inability or total lack of desire to relate to people of the opposite sex."[3] It is dangerous for a person who has been sexually molested as a minor to consider himself homosexual, for he plays into the hands of the "gay" community and opens himself to exploitation by homosexuals.

It saddens me to think of the number of people who are homosexuals and lesbians today. I have talked with many of them, and every one told me he first became involved in homosexuality when he was approached by a homosexual. Some named contributing factors, such as a weak father or a smothering mother.

In January, 1977, Anita Bryant and her husband Bob Green, along with fifty other Miami citizens, stepped out in opposition to a proposed ordinance, which, among other things, would have allowed known, practicing homosexuals to teach in private and religious schools. Immediately they were embroiled in a dramatic and emotional struggle with militant homosexuals, which hasn't stopped since. The Miami dispute erupted into a full-blown national issue. In her two books written since that event, Anita lays open her heart as she reveals the true story. The media has slanted and distorted the events and Anita and Bob's responses to them. Through it all, this young couple has stood firm on biblical principles, declaring at all times that they love the sinner but hate the sin. They are standing on solid ground. When the Lord spoke to Moses, He plainly declared that Moses was to tell the people "Thou shalt not lie with mankind, as with womankind: it is abomination" (Lev. 18:22). What could be plainer?

There are those who try to explain away their deviant sexual impulses by saying they were born with them and, therefore, can't help themselves. There is much disagreement about this theory among medical scientists. The *Miami Herald* medical writer did an article entitled "Origins of Homosexuality Elude Scientists' Inquiry." Indeed! Has anyone ever been able to pinpoint sin under a microscope or isolate it in some lab? *Sin is sin.*

Even the American Psychiatric Association, which for years explained that homosexuality was "a sexual deviation" ranked with sadism, masochism, and fetishism, has removed it from its list of mental disorders. Now, a growing number of psychiatrists say that homosexuality *per se* is not an illness nor an inherited condition but is a chosen life-style.

Our present permissive culture can never provide the Christian's guideline; we must stand on the Word of God. The Word does not endorse homosexuality or adopt even a neutral stance.

The "Gay" Revolution

Never in recorded history has there been such a rapid decline in moral standards in the Western world as we are seeing in this generation. So-called "gay power" is exerting itself in our cities and making inroads into government and business. The gay lobbyists are working on this nation's sympathies by asserting that gays are the second largest minority group in the country.

Even in some churches, this practice, condemned in Scriptures, is now accepted. Some religious leaders prefer to be silent on the issue. They whisper to each other that homosexuality is wrong, but they refuse to take a stand. They silently hope the issue won't rear its head in their churches. Others acquiesce, saying "Let's just accept them and hope for the best."

The Christian Response

A homosexual cannot function unless he persuades another person to be a homosexual also. A lesbian must find another woman in order to carry out her base, shameful deeds. The Christian world cannot sit idly by if it values its children's well-being and if it wants for them a healthy, wholesome environment. The Bible presents the truth about homosexuality, no matter what the laws of this country say. Sodom and Gomorrah probably had such laws also, but that did not stop God's hail of fire from destroying those places. What God ordains will be; we must listen to Him. The sexual revolution now going on in our nation is godless, contrary to the Bible, and an enemy of the family. It is an attack upon everything sacred. Jesus prophesied that this evil would appear in great proportions in the latter days, before His judgment of the world. Now, because we see such an immoral world, we must pay careful attention to this trend.

The Bible refers to the human body as the temple of the Holy Spirit. The body is precious to God. ". . . Know ye not," wrote Paul, "that your body is the temple of the Holy Ghost which is in you, which ye have of God, and ye are not your own? For ye are bought with a price . . ." (1 Cor. 6:19, 20). God does not dwell in a temple built by human hands; He wants to dwell in our bodies. Obviously He is not going to be pleased to dwell in a body that is impure, that engages in shameful acts, that works against normal, natural laws.

There are those today who say that the Bible's teachings on chastity, virginity, and morality are harmful. They argue that if we are to go by the Bible, the results will be frustration, anxiety, inhibitions, and mental disturbances. They tell us that to rid ourselves of these frustrations and what they call "guilt complexes," we must "do our own thing."

In response, Dr. James Kennedy, pastor of Coral Ridge Presbyterian Church in Fort Lauderdale, Florida, speaks of two people with different life-styles. One of them, a man, says that he did not even kiss his wife until after he was engaged to her. The other person, a woman, says she has had frequent sexual relations outside of marriage.

Some psychologists would tell us, Dr. Kennedy suggests, that the life-style of the man should surely send him to a mental institution and that the woman should be well-adjusted and mentally healthy. But actually the reverse is true. The man spoken of is Billy Graham, obviously one of the happiest people in the world. The woman is an inmate in the Broward County Mental Hospital in Florida. Overwhelmed with a guilt complex so great that her mind gave way, she had to be placed in the hospital.

Since the Garden of Eden, the devil has whispered to humanity, "Don't listen to God; He will hurt you. If you listen to Him, you will be narrow-minded and unhappy." The sooner we discover this is a lie, the better. We know better than to jump off the roof of a house. God's universal laws operate along lines as predictable as the law of gravity. When we break moral laws, our moral fiber is broken.

God will not force His will upon us, but those who choose the homosexual life-style take the law into their own hands. When Eve ate the forbidden fruit, it brought her shame, fear, humiliation, guilt, sickness, and eventual death. When you and I eat of the forbidden fruit of sexual immorality, we can look forward to the same.

How Do You Cope?

Deviant sex is a special problem within the larger scope of our sexual behavior. What I offer here is specific advice for persons whose sex lives are abnormally oriented, who seem incapable of channeling their sex drives into normal, heterosexual relationships.

I am absolutely convinced that there is hope for anyone who wants to bring his or her deviant sexual orientation around to normal expression. How quickly a person can expect a change depends on many things. If a girl has had few homosexual experiences and genuinely wants to change, she can expect a more rapid deliverance than the girl who has lived as an active lesbian for a number of years. The level of desire for change is an important factor also, for a homosexual will have to overthrow much of his life in order to change. He may have to change his place of lodging, and most certainly he will have to end friendships with homosexuals. His recreational activities, the books he reads, the movies he watches—these will all have to be evaluated. If they hinder his progress toward a normal sex life or make him susceptible to temptation, he must be willing to make the necessary changes.

The most surprising statistic in the latest Masters and Johnson research on sex, according to *Time* magazine, is that a majority of homosexuals who seek treatment successfully revert to heterosexuality. Between 1968 and 1971, Masters and Johnson found that of 151 individuals who wanted to be heterosexuals, more than half were successful in their change.[4]

But what of those who were unsuccessful? We do not know if any of them were introduced to God and to the power available through His Son Jesus Christ. This is crucial. The first question I ask of people who come to me with this problem is "Do you know Jesus Christ?" I seek to lead a person first to Christ, and if he believes he is a Christian already, I ask him to make Christ king in his life. Self must leave the throne.

God does not work in all our lives in the same way. I have heard former alcoholics testify that in giving themselves to Christ they lost their thirst for alcohol completely. The homosexual might find a similar transformation in his own life.

More common is the gradual healing and change that come to the homosexual or lesbian who battles for a period of time before he or she sees a definite change taking place. Some find that they are never free of the temptation to deviate into homosexual behavior; for them, as for many reformed alcoholics, situations that could contribute to their downfall must be avoided.

Discipline Your Inner Urgings

If you have a deviant urge, immediately turn to God. He can give you strength to curb your inner drives and will give you victory as you seek to be obedient to Him.

It is important to associate with those who can help you strengthen your resolve to break your old ways. Dissociate yourself totally from those in the gay movement. Ask the Lord to give you someone with whom you can discuss your innermost feelings and with whom you can pray. Enter into the life of the church. Take part in some form of regular Bible study, and do what you can to make friends within the body of Christ. This fellowship will aid you in prayer; the activities and recreation will fill lonely hours when you might otherwise be tempted to fall back into the old life.

Resist the Devil

The Bible says, ". . . Resist the devil, and he will flee . . ." (James 4:7). If necessary, vocally resist Satan; call out his name, and command his evil spirit to go. Take charge of your life, under Christ the King. An alcoholic who is trying not to drink does not keep a bottle of wine under his pillow; neither does a "clean" addict leave drugs lying around. You too are fighting to overcome an enslavement, and part of the way you resist Satan is by avoiding the places where you are likely to meet with temptation. On the positive side, you can fortify yourself by studying the Bible and memorizing God's Word.

The church can aid you. Seek out a minister or a fellow Christian who will offer you unconditional love and at the same time will *help lift you toward God's standard of righ-*

teous living. Ask others to join you in the prayer of deliverance. I have laid hands on men and women who have been possessed by the evil spirit of deviant sex, and the spirit has left. These people have found peace.

If you know of a Christian ministry devoted to the "gay" community, seek it out. Often you will meet other former homosexuals who can offer you a sympathetic ear and support. If you do not know of such a local ministry, write to Spatula Ministries, Box 444, La Habra, California 90631. This group can help you, or put you in contact with a ministry closer to you.

Barbara Johnson, founder of this ministry, is the mother of a homosexual. When she learned of her son's homosexual activities, her heart was broken. In despair she sought help from others who had experienced what she was going through, but she couldn't find such help. "Where were all the other parents who were suffering through this thing?" she wondered. Spatula Ministries exists to help parents, other family members, friends, and the church respond to homosexuals and lesbians in God-honoring, loving ways.

You can also contact Anita Bryant and Bob Green at their ministry headquarters. Write to Protect America's Children, P.O. Box 402745, Miami Beach, Florida 33140. Their outreach to homosexuals and lesbians is growing, as God blesses these efforts.

Sex Education in the Home

I strongly recommend that parents provide sex education for their children. Many children do not learn about sex, pregnancy, and birth control at home; they learn about it elsewhere, often picking up wrong ideas and warped concepts in the process.

The home is the proper place for sex education, but it is obvious that many parents neglect this duty. If we wait for the schools to teach our children, we will not be pleased either. The schools must be neutral on religious matters; very often they refuse God's Word as a standard, and their advice reflects liberal views and is contrary to the Word.

The church can help guide young people into wholesome sexual concepts by reinforcing what parents teach. Refusing to give proper sex education is like refusing a child pure drinking water. We would not tell our children to take a drink from the gutter, yet, in effect, millions of children are drinking stagnant water because their parents have not or will not teach them moral standards.

Remember—Homosexuals Are Persons Needing Love

A final word is necessary, especially to individuals who consider themselves normal in regard to sexual expression. Sometimes we are not very loving toward those who are homosexual. In our rage against this evil, we are not always willing to listen to homosexuals. We show them revulsion rather than love. Perhaps this is because we aren't quite sure how to handle the subject, so we walk away from it in embarrassment. Rather than risk embarrassment to self and to the homosexual, we do not offer love and friendship. By our attitude and rejection (for no sin is worse than any other in God's eyes), we have driven homosexuals away. We have contributed to their desperate loneliness. That is not Christ's way. In this area of life, it is important that we extend loving friendship, a sympathetic ear, a body of fellowship. Christ calls us to be agents of His redeeming love. Remember the words of James: "Let him know, that he which converteth the sinner from the error of his way shall save a soul from death, and shall hide a multitude of sins" (James 5:20).

There is help and hope for all those involved in deviant sexual practices. If the Christian world and the church do not extend love to such as these, they will seek it elsewhere, continuing their immoral practices. God forbid that you and I should be guilty of encouraging immorality by our failure to help those who need help.

[1]*Psychology Today, An Introduction,* 2nd ed. (Del Mar, Calif.: CRM Books, 1970), p. 604.
[2]"How Gay Is Gay?" *Time* (Apr. 23, 1979), p. 72.
[3]*HIS* magazine, (Mar. 1979), p. 13.
[4]"How Gay Is Gay?" p. 72.

10

Advancing Age and Retirement: The Best Is Yet to Be

William Feather once said, "Some people are making such thorough preparation for rainy days that they aren't enjoying today's sunshine."

This is the sad commentary on some who look only to the future. Occasionally we hear of the death of an elderly person who is found destitute, malnourished, and ill. Under the mattress, under the carpet, or occasionally in a savings account are found thousands, and even millions, of dollars belonging to these apparently indigent aged.

One kindly old gentleman, a dentist, practiced dentistry five days a week, walking to and from his office, until he was ninety-two years old. His "retirement" years included a yearly trip from east Texas to Tennessee to visit his brother. He enjoyed people and life. He kept his keen mind and sense of humor until his death—five months before his one-hundred-second birthday.

On the other hand, there was the great grandmother who, for ninety-two years, lived a life of resentment, self-pity, and selfishness. When she could no longer care for herself in her home, her children provided for her care in a nursing home. Although her children and their families visited when they could and she was lovingly remembered with gifts, her heart was so full of bitterness, she spent each visit demeaning the family members not present. Her bitterness and resentment so hardened her heart that she was not aware who was visiting with her nor of the gifts they had sent. She became obsessed with those who *didn't* visit her and with those who (in her mind) had failed to send her a gift.

A little lady in Albany, Georgia, who will be one hundred if she lives until 1983, is continuing to live a full life. Mary Moore was converted in 1897, at age fourteen, and commenced a life of Christian service. For many years she taught Sunday school, worked in the Ladies Aid Society and the Foreign Mission Society, and reviewed books.

"I memorized a Bible verse a week for a long time," she says. She helped many discouraged people through these Scripture passages. She passed along many little booklets with Bible solutions to difficult problems that people faced.

When she became a shut-in a few years ago, she began to minister from her room in a nursing home. Her own spirit received nourishment from Christian radio and television programs and tapes. When her eyes gave out, she had her daughter read books to her.

In 1978 she said, "Each morning I pray that God will allow me to minister and not just be ministered to. I want to give and be useful." She does give; she is able to minister to many visitors who come to her room—an average of about five a week—and even ministers to her clergy friends.

She misses being able to prepare lessons to teach. "I had my book of illustrations and my book of poems which I used along with the lessons. Many times a poem would say just the right thing." Her favorite verse is Isaiah 41:10—"Fear thou not; for I am with thee: be not dismayed; for I am thy God: I will strengthen thee; yea, I will help thee; yea, I will uphold thee with the right hand of my righteousness."

Some of the greatest feats ever accomplished were performed by those in their seventies and eighties.

Moses led the children of Israel for forty years. He was eighty when he began and one hundred and twenty when he went to heaven. (Deut. 34:7). He was a mighty man who did not become ill before death. When his time was up, he went to be with God.

Joshua conquered the land of promise when he was past eighty and died at one hundred and ten.

At age eighty-five Caleb was chasing giants, the three sons of Anak, down the Judean hills. He was as strong at eighty-five as he had been at forty (Josh. 14:7–11).

Longfellow wrote:

> Ah, nothing is too late,
> Till the tired heart shall cease to palpitate.
> Cato learned Greek at eighty; Sophocles
> Wrote his grand Oedipus, and Simonides
> Bore off the prize of verse from his compeers,
> When each had numbered more than fourscore years.[1]

Few men have shaped this world for God like John Wesley. Note this entry from his *Journal:*

Saturday, June 28. I enter this day on my 85th year; and what cause have I to praise God, as for a thousand spiritual blessings, so for bodily blessings also? How little have I suffered yet, by "the rush of numerous years." It is true, I am not so agile as I was in times past . . . I find, likewise, some decay in my memory, with regard to names, and things lately passed, but not at all with regard to what I have read or heard, 20, 40, or 60 years ago. Neither do I find any decay in my hearing, smell, taste, or appetite . . . nor do I feel any such thing as weariness, either in traveling or preaching; and I am not conscious of any decay in writing sermons, which I do as readily, and I believe as correctly, as ever.

To what cause can I impute this, that I am as I am? First, doubtless, to the power of God, fitting me for the work to which I am called, as long as he pleases to continue me therein; and next, subordinately, to this, to the prayers of his children.

May we not impute it, as inferior means, 1) To my constant exercise and change of air? 2) To my having sleep at command, so that whenever I feel myself almost worn out, I call it, and it comes, day or night? 3) To my having constantly, for above 60 years, risen at four in the morning? 4) To my constant preaching at five in the morning, for above 50 years?[2]

You can determine *now* how meaningful your later years will be. You can simply "exist," waiting for death, or you can live every moment of every day to the fullest. "Society cannot make you a dignified, interesting person. It is something you must do for yourself—like getting your own haircut—nobody can do it for you."[3]

A seventy-five-year-old man was recently elected mayor of a small Texas community he had earlier served as judge. His retirement years had been filled with meaningful activities: raising Black Angus cows, stocking a lake with fish, paving country roads, and writing several genealogical books.

But his decision to make life interesting didn't come suddenly. In his fifties he served as deputy sheriff, learned on his own to read and speak Spanish, and went deer hunting annually. At age fifty-five, he learned to fly an airplane, got his pilot's license, and purchased his own plane.

You may say, "Yes, but he had money to do all that." You are right; he made his millions in the Texas oil fields. But, even in that, he knew early what he wanted to do in life, so he made money in order to be able to do those things.

Preparing for Old Age

Growing old is a natural part of living. In America, especially, old age is considered a sentence of doom passed on those unfortunate souls who live too long. Our society is youth-oriented. We push aside the old so as not to be reminded that age comes to us all. "Out of sight; out of mind," as the saying goes.

But we can arrive at old age with respect and dignity and, therefore, not be pushed aside by the young. As Cicero said, "Old age, especially an honored old age, has so great authority, that it is of more value than all the pleasures of youth."[4]

Philip Yancey wrote in his book *Where Is God When It Hurts?*:

The best way to prepare for a crisis is to have a strong, supportive life when you're healthy. Mental suffering and physical pain merely warn us of a problem; they are characteristics of disease, not the disease itself. You cannot suddenly fabricate foundations of strength from nowhere; they must have been building all along. If you learn a pattern of depending on others and sharing yourself when healthy, it will be a more natural response when you're in pain.

A common illustration of that process is seen in the diverse ways people prepare for old age, a period of great psychological suffering. There is an old saying, "The young get the face they are born with; the old get the face they deserve." The life we have lived crystallizes into the less flexible personality of old age.[5]

What are some of the desirable attributes we can bring to old age?

Love. God's love in our lives enables us to love the unlovely and love our enemies—those who provoke and annoy. God's love is unconditional, given without the expectation of anything in return. It is esteem for a human being, sympathy, compatibility, care and affection, and friendship. Love turns off hate, revenge, grudges, bitterness, and resentment in our lives.

Joy. The person who has found delight, happiness, cheerfulness, gladness, and pleasure in living is easy to be around. Joy is optimism, good humor, and a sense of humor. The joyful, light heart is a heart free of the burdens and cares of living. It comes through confession of sin and repentance and through giving all our worries to Jesus (1 Pet. 5:7).

Peace. Peace is calmness, serenity, and quietness despite the uncertainty, confusion, and disorder all around. It means being a peacemaker when one is needed. It means being cooperative and neutral. (Thou shalt not take sides.) It is mature silence amid the turmoil.

Patience. Patience is the ability to bear pain or trials without complaining. Patience is tolerance—of other people, of their life-styles, mannerisms, ideas, weaknesses. It is tolerance of ourselves—of our own failures and limitations; it is acceptance of the consequences of our own choices. Patience is evidenced by an even, long-suffering temperament that stands firm despite opposition or adversity.

Kindness. Warmth of heart, generosity, benevolence, loving-kindness, and kind deeds are all components of kindness. The ability to sympathize is another important aspect. *You and Your Aging Parent* states,

Our attitudes vary, depending on whether we admire old people or secretly despise them, whether we feel older people deserve respect or consideration, whether we believe they can remain sexually or creatively active, whether we dread the day when we will be old or the day we will die . . . The feelings we have about our own old age often have a direct bearing on how effectively we can help our parents during their old age, and how constructively we can plan for our own.

People who have a generally positive attitude toward old age in general—including their own—are more likely to be able to reach out to their elderly parents with concern, compassion, and constructive support. If old age appears as a time to be dreaded—and many features of modern society would suggest to us that it is—then our parents' decline may seem very threatening. Their aging seems to toll the bells for our own aging and our inevitable death.[6]

Goodness. Goodness differs from kindness in that kindness is the goodness shown others, whereas goodness is a virtue of the soul from which proceed righteousness, integrity, morality, and honesty.

Faithfulness. Being loyal, conscientious, incorruptible, trustworthy, and true to one's word are virtues of the faithful.

Gentleness. Tender, merciful, polite, thoughtful, well-mannered, meek, well-behaved, humble, mild—these are the attributes of gentleness.

Self-control. This is the real test of one's mettle. Self-restraint, self-discipline, willpower, patience are indicators of the real strength of a character.

Self-control means perseverance, the ability to keep on when the way is difficult, painful, unpleasant, or unending. Self-control means bridling our tongues—not giving advice unless asked for it. It means restraining ourselves from taking matters into our own hands and allowing others to learn by their own mistakes and experiences, while we refrain from suggesting they do as we did in similar situations.

If these attributes seem familar, they are called the "fruit of the Spirit" in Galatians 5:22,23.

Retirement

Charles Barrows said,

You know that life is something like a book. When you come to the end of a chapter you have two choices: you can go back and reread the chapter you have just finished or turn the page and see what exciting things are ahead. I have found that it is a lot more interesting to turn the page.[7]

Retirement can be the beginning of a new chapter in your life. Face yourself anew, and be courageous enough to explore some new aspect of yourself. Pursue those interests you had no time for earlier. Enroll in a class to learn a new

135

skill. Serve as a volunteer in an organization that needs you. Be a "grandparent" for those who do not have grandparents nearby. If you enjoy plants and flowers and are good with them, work part-time in a flower shop.

Retirement can be the time you finally read the Bible through, or study in depth some portion of Scripture, or visit the sick and the newcomers in town. Just because you are getting older does not mean that the Lord is diminishing His working in your life. He may have a *new* gift He wants you to have and use.

Many retired persons are finding that God uses the skills of their vocations to further His work. They are going to the mission field to teach school; be house parents; minister medically; construct buildings; be agricultural consultants; install computers, telephone equipment, and generators; to ready airplanes and facilities for service; and to be accountants, secretaries, or bookkeepers.

Ann Landers gives a few examples of second careers:

A retired businessman, long fascinated by animals, conducts tours at the zoo. He specializes in grade-school classes, helping children develop a sense of wonder. A cavalry officer at age ninety-one is still teaching young people how to jump hunters in a horse show. A retired accountant took a course in income tax law and returned home to teach what he had learned to sixteen other accountants.[8]

On the other hand, there are those who, having received the gold watch and the farewell dinner, now have unlimited leisure time. This freedom becomes a burden, because they are bored. So, they tamper with the already organized, well-functioning lives of their wives. As the humorous saying goes, "She died of a retired husband."

Life has lost its meaning for these people, who lock themselves in a jail of self-imposed confinement and throw away the keys. They rock back and forth in their rocking chairs, rereading the previous chapters of their lives, or they slouch before their television sets. A world in need passes them by; a world struggling for existence deteriorates before their lonely eyes, and they deteriorate with it.

Grace Halsell visited an isolated village known as Sacred Valley in the rugged Andean mountains of southern Ecuador. In Sacred Valley live *los viejos*—those who live exceptionally long lives, some up to one-hundred-thirty-two years. She went there hoping to find the secret of their longevity. In her book, *Los Viejos,* she records her discoveries.

The people of Sacred Valley were puzzled by her interest in how *long* they lived. They enjoyed life and the living of life, so they could not understand the emphasis on duration.

They live by certain "truths," reported Halsell. The first truth is that "health is not a commodity that you can buy at a corner drugstore or get from a high-priced doctor."[9] They live close to nature, see no doctors, and take no pills. Their healthful living habits exclude smoking, drinking, white sugar, and white flour.

The second truth is that "you can live out your life taking care of yourself, dressing yourself, making your own bed, preparing your meals, being self-sufficient."[10] The *viejos* never worry about being put in nursing homes, being without friends, being alone, helpless, or degraded. They take care of themselves as long as they live.

The third truth is that "you have two 'doctors'—your left leg and your right leg."[11] Everyday the old ones climb a steep mountain to tend their gardens and to fetch water. This is their exercise.

The fourth truth is that "you can eat much less beef—and still get all the protein you need."[12] The *viejos* get their protein from cheese, vegetables, and nuts, since they eat almost no beef. They eat "pure" fresh foods, with no chemicals, no additives, and they get their vitamins in the natural foods they eat.

The fifth truth is that "you can grow as old as Erazo (132) but you need not grow senile."[13] Like the *viejos*, we need to meet new challenges every day. At Duke University, longevity study tests show that "those who keep using their brains don't lose their capacity, that a seventy- or eighty-year-old can think as well as anyone, provided he has kept his mind occupied."[14]

There is in our society one other area of aging that is no problem to the *viejos* but that we must consider—finances. Begin early in life putting aside money for retirement. Make allowance for the type of life-style you want, where you want to live, inflation, and other unforseen circumstances that can eat away at your nest egg.

Why Old Age?

Philip Yancey writes in his book,

J. Robertson McQuilkin, president of Columbia Bible College, was once approached by an elderly lady facing these trials. "Robertson, why does God let us get old and weak? Why must I hurt so?" she asked him.

"After a few moments' thought he replied, "I think God has planned the strength and beauty of youth to be physical. But the strength and beauty of age is spiritual. We gradually lose the strength and beauty that is temporary so we'll be sure to concentrate on the strength and beauty which is forever. And so we'll be eager to leave the temporary, deteriorating part of us and be truly homsesick for our eternal home. If we stayed young and strong and beautiful, we might never want to leave!"[15]

---

[1]Henry Wadsworth Longfellow, *Morituri Salutamus* (1875), stanza 22 as quoted in *Familiar Quotations*, John Bartlett, (Boston: Little, Brown and Co., 1955), p. 525.

[2]*The Journal of John Wesley*, ed. Percy L. Parker (Chicago: Moody Press, 1974), p. 405.

[3]*The Ann Landers Encyclopedia A to Z* (Garden City, New York: Double-day, 1978), p. 47.

[4]Marcus Tullius Cicero, *De Senectute. XVII,* as quoted in *Familiar Quotations,* John Bartlett, p. 34.

[5]Philip Yancey, *Where Is God When It Hurts?* (Grand Rapids, Mich.: Zondervan 1977), p. 155.

[6]Barbara Silverstone and Helen Kandel Hyman, *You and Your Aging Parent* (New York: Pantheon Books, 1976), pp. 26–27.

[7]Helen Kooiman Hosier, *Profiles: People Who Are Helping to Change the World* (New York: Hawthorne Books, 1977), p. 7–8.

[8]*The Ann Landers Encyclopedia,* p. 47.

[9]Grace Halsell, *Los Viejos* (Emmaus, Penn: Rodale Press, 1976), p. 175.

[10]*Ibid.,* p. 176.

[11]*Ibid.*

[12]*Ibid.*

[13]*Ibid.,* p. 177

[14]*Ibid.*

[15]Yancey, *Where Is God When It Hurts?,* p. 155.

11
Making Good Your Grief

The one you love has died. Family, friends, and clergy are there to offer comfort and strength in your time of grief.

But what if you are grieving when no one has died? Perhaps a relationship has died or you have suffered some other great loss, or you are sorrowing over another's condition. The grief is real. Yet, no one seems to recognize *your* need for comfort, support, and encouragement.

This chapter is written for those who are suffering grief, no matter what the cause.

Stages of Grief

There are stages in the grief process.

The grief process is the movement through which one lives as one experiences the loss day by day. Hopefully it is a healing process as one goes from one stage to another. It must be emphasized that grief is not pathological but a healthy response to the ebb and flow of life.[1]

The immediate reaction when faced with unexpected death is usually one of shock or numbness. This reaction also occurs in those who have obtained a divorce or in those whose loved ones have overdosed on drugs, succumbed to the devastation of alcoholism, been severely injured, been arrested, or been diagnosed as terminally ill. According to *Today's Health Guide,* "This state of shock is helpful to him because he does not have to comprehend all at once the magnitude of his loss."[2]

During this period of shock and numbness, Franklin Segler observes,

You are not fully aware of what is going on. It does not seem real. You cannot meet the responsibilities of the next few hours. Don't be afraid of your feelings. They are normal . . . . Simply be aware that your emotions are in shock, and don't be too frustrated and disturbed about it all.[3]

This is the time when you need to be ministered to by those who care. You may be so anesthetized by your grief that you forget you have children depending on you to meet their needs. Let the children be taken by someone who will lovingly care for them. Let others provide meals and attend to needs. If a funeral must be arranged, allow others to assist in working out details. (It is wise for any of us to write in detail, sign, and put in a safe place, what we wish done for our funeral. Then, when loved ones are in this initial state of shock, they do not have to try to remember the wishes of the deceased.)

According to *Today's Health Guide,* "The second stage of grief is emotional release. This comes about the time it begins to dawn on the person how dreadful his loss is."[4] This is facing up to the reality of what has happened. "There is no way to avoid the pain of it. It is a healthy pain that brings its own healing. Accept the fact that your loved one is dead. Go ahead and cry. Express as much grief as you feel."[5]

"Many people appear to have the impression that a person who has a mature religious faith should not grieve . . . They have confused a stoic attitude toward life with religious faith.''⁶ They use ''. . .sorrow not'' (1 Thess. 4:13) as the basis for their assumption that we are not to express our grief. But the verse continues, ''. . .sorrow not, even as others which have no hope.'' If the deceased was a believer in Jesus, then there is no need to sorrow as if his death was the absolute end. He has gone to be with his Savior. He will be resurrected at the Rapture. That is our hope.

It is not a sign of immature faith, therefore, to grieve. There are many heroes of faith listed in Hebrews 11. Many of them suffered much and experienced grief—Jacob was alienated from his family and had to run for his life; Jacob grieved for his son Joseph whom he thought had been eaten by a wild beast; Joseph was beaten by his own brothers, sold as a slave, unjustly lied about, and imprisoned in a dungeon; Moses grieved for the children of Israel, who suffered affliction at the hand of the Egyptians, and he grieved because of their disobedience.

The Bible records those who expressed their grief. David had great sorrow: Saul sought to kill him; his best friend Jonathan was killed; he committed adultery and murder; his baby son died; his son Absalom ran away from home and formed a revolutionary coup against him. The Bible records that at the news of Absalom's death,

. . . the king [David] was much moved, and went up to the chamber over the gate, and wept: and as he went, thus he said, O my son Absalom, my son, my son Absalom! would God I had died for thee, O Absalom, my son, my son! (2 Sam. 18:33).

In Psalm 6:7,8 David says, ''Mine eye is consumed because of grief . . . the Lord hath heard the voice of my weeping.''

Other biblical accounts of weeping in sorrow and grief are related with moving impact.

143

Can you imagine the grief of the mothers of the children, two years old and under, who were killed by Herod. "In Rama was there a voice heard, lamentation, and weeping, and great mourning, Rachel weeping for her children, and would not be comforted, because they are not" (Matt. 2:18).

Jesus and others wept at the tomb of Lazarus who had died. "When Jesus therefore saw her weeping, and the Jews also weeping which came with her, he groaned in the spirit, and was troubled . . . Jesus wept" (John 11:33,35).

Mary wept, distressed because she could not find the dead body of Jesus. "But Mary stood without at the sepulchre weeping: and as she wept, she stooped down, and looked into the sepulchre" (John 20:11).

Friends of Dorcas mourned this good woman whose life was spent doing kind deeds for the poor. In her room ". . . all the widows stood by him weeping, and shewing the coats and garments which Dorcas made, while she was with them" (Acts 9:39).

Another stage of grief is pining. This is "an intense wish to get the dead person back in some form or other" as stated in an article on death and dying.[7] Pining is also experienced by those who wish that a relationship for which they grieve could be as it was in happier times.

Although the struggle to seek out the dead person [or afflicted person or relationship] is ultimately futile, this does not stop people from going to places and treasuring objects associated with the deceased. Nor does it prevent the survivors from going over in their minds the events that led up to the loss as if, even now, they could discover what went wrong and put it aright.

At times bereaved people will even experience a strong sense of the presence of the deceased.[8]

This was illustrated in the Billy Graham movie *For Pete's Sake*. The young wife and mother had died, and the grieving father was trying to prepare a meal for his son. Each time he stepped into the kitchen, visions of his wife immobilized him. Everything he saw reminded him of his wife.

Others have similar memories: the divorceé, fingering her engagement ring, remembers her happiness the night her ex-husband proposed to her; the mother grieving for her child, who is now on drugs, or in prison, or injured, or terminally ill, remembers the happiness of his childhood. Because of these pangs of grief, some people get rid of everything that reminds them of less painful times. "Psychiatric evidence indicates that, far from preventing grief, such attempts only postpone. When grief that has been delayed in this way does begin to emerge, it will be more painful and disruptive than grief that has been fully expressed at the time of loss."[9] We should cherish our memories without allowing them to bind us to the past.

The next stage in grief is one of "utter depression, loneliness, and a sense of isolation. The person feels that there is no help for him. He is down in the depths of despair; nothing could be so awful as his depression."[10] He feels what the prophet Jeremiah expressed in Lamentations 1:12, "Is it nothing to you, all ye that pass by? behold, and see if there be any sorrow like unto my sorrow, which is done unto me, wherewith the Lord hath afflicted me in the day of his fierce anger."

This is a normal reaction to grief. The grieving person may become apathetic and feel that life has no more meaning. Those who have already worked through their grief can be a comfort during this time. Empathy from one who has overcome grief can be of some comfort.

Closely akin to this stage of grief is the grieving person's panic about his obsession with his own grief. He wonders if he will ever overcome his grief, if he will ever be able to think about anything besides his loss, if he is losing his mind. Hannah must have experienced this. In telling Eli why she

145

was praying with such expression, she tried to explain that she was praying "out of the abundance of her . . . grief" (1 Sam. 1:16). Her heart was overwhelmed with grief.

Grief may bring physical symptoms. One woman I know suddenly became so weak it was necessary for her to go to bed. For several days she had no strength even to eat; it was as if her entire energy system had been shut down.

Gradually she regained her strength enough to go to the doctor. He told her, "Your body is suffering from grief. Has someone close to you recently died?" She assured him no one had. He said, "Are you sure you are not grieving? Your body is crying out in grief. I don't understand why, when you say you are not grieving." He prescribed that she rest when she felt her strength going. He advised that it might be a long time before she regained her strength.

What this woman would not share with her doctor was the sorrow she felt because of her husband. He was a good man, but he did not share her love for and interest in the Lord and His Word. She ministered to college students by teaching the Bible, but her husband resented this and did not encourage her in it in any way.

At one time or another a person usually experiences feelings of guilt about everything related to his loss. He may begin to "ruminate over his own mistakes which may have contributed to the significant loss or reversal. He has a tendency at that point to blame himself for everything. Hindsight is always better than foresight; he can see in hindsight things he could have done that *may* have helped prevent the loss."[11]

This is the time the grieving person is usually plagued with "if only." The reality is, this sad event *did* happen, and the person must change what he can to insure against it happening again. He must press onward, never looking back again at the condemning finger of "if only."

This is usually the phase when the one in grief asks, "What sin have I committed to merit this punishment?" As he surveys his suffering, he concludes that God must be responsible, so he turns on God.

"Why did this have to happen to me? What have I done more than others to deserve this? Why this? Couldn't it have been something else? Why now? Just when everything was going so well."

If this stage of grief is prolonged, the grieving one becomes impatient. "When are you going to remove this? It's not fair! Are you enjoying my suffering? I can't stand it any longer."

After the one who is suffering resolves his hostility, he may try to return to his usual activities. Often he finds he is unable to, because his grief is still as sensitive as a fresh scar. But those around him seem to want to forget that anything ever happened. They offer comfort at the funeral (or at the divorce court, at the hospital, at jail), but after that they seem to say, "Let's get back to business as usual." In America we make it difficult for people to grieve openly. We expect that by the time a person is ready for usual activities, he should be over "all that grieving."

Joni Eareckson admonishes, "We should never be alone when we suffer. I don't mean never for a minute, or that we must not live in an apartment by ourselves. But we should never build a self-imposed wall around us that allows absolutely no one inside to see what we're going through and to hurt with our hurts. God never intended that we shoulder the load of suffering by ourselves."[12] "Two are better than one. . . . For if they fall, the one will lift up his fellow: but woe to him that is alone when he falleth; for he hath not another to help him up" (Eccles. 4:9,10).

At the last stage, we readjust our lives to reality. The last stage is not "we are our old selves again." We are never our old selves again after we have had a great grief experience. We are different from what we were before. But we believe that we can be stronger people and deeper people, and better able to help others because of what we have experienced.[13]

147

Now we are ready to plan for the future. We can discover new interests and activities. We can make new acquaintances and develop new relationships.

The Eye Opener

During each stage of grief we try to fit all the pieces together and make sense out of the experience. Like Job, we ask God to explain the meaning of all that is happening. We feel that God is hiding His face from us, not seeing or caring what is happening to us (Job 23:3–5). We remind ourselves how much He loves us, but then, in our own minds, the grief becomes larger to us than His love.

We are encouraged by and blessed with many special "little" things that are just for us. In these we get a glimpse of the love of God, but we begin to grieve again because the apparent meaninglessness of our loss overshadows everything.

We cry to the Lord to deliver us from our blindness to His ways and to help us take everything as from His hand. Yet, when He begins to show "good" that has come from our affliction, we sometimes feel that no "good" could compensate for our grief.

Then, at God's appointed time, our eyes are opened to see that:

(1) He is our heavenly Father who truly loves us. He will be with us no matter what comes (Heb. 12:5–9; Ps. 139:17,18; Jer. 9:24; Isa. 43:2,3; Ps. 138:7; Ps. 34:18,19; Ps. 46:1).

(2) *Everything* that we suffer, Jesus has already suffered for us (Isa. 53:4; 1 Pet. 2:21).

(3) What grief He allows in our lives is custom-made for us by His loving hands (Job 23:14).

(4) We must not try to understand our suffering or His ways, but must trust Him completely. (Deut. 8:2; Isa. 55:8; Rom. 11:33; Ps. 18:30).

(5) What grief we experience is not because we are being punished for our sin. Jesus dealt with our sin at Calvary. After we trust Him for salvation, we must confess our sin to daily keep our Christian lives cleansed (1 John 1:9). But the Lord is never out to punish us for our sins. He has paid the penalty for our sins (Mark 10:45; Rom. 3:23–25).

Some of God's people have led us to believe that His will for us as spiritual Christians is always to be wealthy, healthy, and beautiful spiritual winners. We are led to believe that if we do not have these attributes, we are not fully committed Christians. This concept is not substantiated in the Word of God. We are exhorted to be overcomers, not sinless saints.

(6) Nothing happens by chance (Job 23:10; Job 34:21; Jer. 29:11; Ps. 37:23,24).

(7) God allows us to suffer that we might learn to trust Him for all that we need—comfort, strength, relief from burdens (Matt. 11:28–30). In Exodus 3:9 He says, ". . .the cry of the children of Israel is come unto me. . . ."

As Edith Schaeffer has pointed out in her book *Affliction,* God has warned us that "trouble will result if we rush for help *away* from God (Isa. 30:1–3). There is an impatience pictured here, a specific walking in the opposite direction, going somewhere for help and advice from a source that is neither the Bible nor the Lord's guidance in answer to prayer."[14]

There are those who, in their hours of grief, blame God for their losses. They vow that if He could cause them that much pain, they want nothing else to do with him. They turn their backs on God and the church, sometimes for the rest of their lives.

Some turn to cults and exotic religious philosophies to find comfort and those who "care" for them. However, God has warned us not to turn away from Him, but to come to Him for comfort and compassion.

(8) The grief and suffering God allows in our lives is to fit us to comfort others (2 Cor. 1:3–7; 1 Cor. 10:11).

149

Joyce Landorf made these observations in her book *The High Cost of Growing:*

> The people acquainted with suffering have this in common: they *rarely* give quick, pat answers. And when they speak, I am aware of the expense and the high cost of their marvelous wisdom.
>
> Those who suffer also have something else in common: they always touch and soothe the spot deep inside me that hurts the most. They have the genuine gift of comforting others.[15]

(9) God wants us to learn to be thankful for everything that comes our way, to praise Him for who He is and not for what He does for us (Ps. 90:15; Isa. 61:3).

In Job 1:10,11 Satan made this accusation to God, ". . . thou hast blessed the work of [Job's] hands, and his substance is increased in the land. But put forth thine hand now, and touch all that he hath, and he will curse thee to thy face." But Job disproved Satan's theory. In Job 13:15, Job says, "Though he slay me, yet will I trust in him. . . ."

Philip Yancey has expressed this idea well in his book *Where is God When it Hurts?.*

> God wants us to freely choose to love Him, even when that choice involves pain—because we are committed to Him, not to our own good feeling and rewards. He wants us to cleave to Him, as Job did, even when we have every reason to hotly deny Him.
>
> That, I believe, is the message of Job. Satan had taunted God with the accusation that humans are not truly free, because God had weighted Job's rewards so he would choose in His favor. Was Job being faithful because God had allowed him such a prosperous life? The test proved he was not. Job is an eternal example of one who stayed faithful to God even though his world caved in and it seemed as though God Himself had turned against him. Job clung to God's justice when, apparently, he was the best example in history of God's alleged injustice. He did not seek the Giver because of His gifts; when all were removed he still sought the Giver.

And so, even in the Old Testament, where suffering is so often identified with God's punishment, the sterling example of Job shines. He endured suffering which he did not deserve to demonstrate that God is ultimately interested in freely given love.[16]

(10) The Lord Jehovah is the only true, holy, sovereign God. He is the Creator of the universe, the Savior of man, King over all other kings; therefore, He has the power, right, and authority to do whatever He pleases (Job 23:13; Isa. 45:9).

(11) The grief God allows in our lives molds us to be more like Christ—to be conformed to his image (Rom. 8:28,29; 5:3–5; James 1:2–4).

Hebrews 12:2 describes Jesus as "the author and finisher of our faith." The primary meaning here is not that of "beginner and ender." It more correctly is translated "creator and refiner" (Mal. 3:2,3).

John A. Hunter describes the refining of silver in his article, "How Should You React When the Heat's On?" In the refining process, a fire is built under the kettle of silver, and the heat is allowed to become more and more intense. "As the heat increases and the silver melts, the imperfections [float] to the top." The impurities are skimmed off.

It may take a long time for the contamination to rise to the top. "The heat may have to be intensified even more to draw the imperfection out. The true test of whether or not the silver is pure is if Christ can see His image when He bends over the silver."[17]

(12) God intends that the ultimate outcome of our grief and suffering will be for "good" and not evil (Gen. 50:20; Rom. 8:28). We should not ask, "*When* can I get out of this?" but "*What* can I get out of this?"

(13) Our suffering and grief will make us more fit for heaven. (2 Cor. 4:17).

Joni Eareckson joyfully says,

Don't you see—when we meet Him face to face, our suffering will have given at least a *tiny* taste of what He went through to purchase our redemption? We will appreciate Him so much more. And our loyalty in those sufferings will give us something to offer Him in return. For what proof could we bring of our love and faithfulness if this life had left us totally unscarred? What shame would we feel if our Christianity had cost us nothing? Suffering prepares us to meet God.[18]

Helping Others Cope with Grief

When we have emerged from our grief somewhat battered, we may be ready to face the realities of life with renewed hope.

Philip Yancey, writing of Psychologist Thomas Malone of the Atlantic Psychiatric Clinic, says that

he meets two kinds of people. One group is unhealthy and studded with inadequacies. These people walk around crying, "Please love me, please love me." The other group is composed of people whole enough to be lovers. He says that the best cure for the first group is to help them to the point where *they* can be lovers and helpers of others. If they reach the place of being helpers, they will automatically fill the deep needs for attention and love inside them.

I think there is a parallel situation among suffering people. Psychiatrists and counselors have found if they can get patients to see themselves as helpers and givers, instead of always receivers, healing may follow.[19]

How can we help those who are experiencing griefs similar to those we have suffered?

Elva McAllaster[20] and Roy Zuck[21] make some suggestions:

Take initiative. Unobtrusively do the little things that mean so much. Help in tangible ways by providing meals and washing dishes afterward, by providing transportation, running errands, or making necessary telephone calls.

Money, included in a meaningful card, could be helpful in some situations. Sit with those who need your company. Potted plants, books, baskets of fruit, stuffed animals, small tins of special teas, games or puzzles may be appropriate gifts in various situations. Ask the Lord to guide in determining the most fitting expression of concern that you can give.

Keep in touch. Whenever and whatever the Holy Spirit prompts you to do, do it. ". . . A word spoken in due season, how good is it!" (Prov. 15:23). Cards, flowers, telephone calls, visits, and Scripture verses are all appreciated at the onslaught of grief. These demonstrations of compassion are a source of healing and encouragement when they are continued.

Listen. Grief needs to be heard. Listen to the memories. Listen not just the first day or first week, but often. Listen, without giving advice, lecturing, or sermonizing.

Remember, you're dealing with amputation. Whether it proceeds from divorce, death, or desertion, our grief results from the loss of vital parts of our lives. We may have made peace with our grief, but we are still amputees.

A young mother whose newborn son had died said to me, "It is never the same. You can have a dozen other children and love them all. Your husband can love you very much. But it is never the same."

Be prayerful about what you say. Job discovered that the silence of his friends was more effective than their speaking. The mere fact of your presence is more meaningful to those in grief than any sage advice you can give.

Don't try to "theologize" with a friend about the purpose of his grief. That's what Job's friends did, and with all their platitudes, they never knew the real story behind Job's suffering.

Don't say, "I know *just* how you feel." You don't. You can't. Every grief is a new and private agony. Remember Jeremiah said, ". . . see if there be any sorrow like unto my sorrow" (Lam. 1:12). Don't assume; don't presume.

153

Don't say, "Time will heal" or "How are you?" or "Do you have other children?" or "Chin up; you've got so much to be thankful for." These statements can cut deep into the wounds of grief.

Don't say the pitying word. Be compassionate and understanding, but not pitying.

Pray. Diligently pray to the Lord for those in grief. Let Him touch them with His own special comfort, strength, peace, and hope.

In some situations, ask what specific needs you can pray for. As Roy Zuck's daughter lay in the hospital, critically injured in an auto collision, loving friends prayed for her specific needs. After prayers were said for her left eye, it began to open. After prayers for her left arm, she began to move it.

The Importance of Friends

Friends are a vital part of overcoming grief and adjusting to a new life after loss.

Special groups have grown out of the members' needs to be with others experiencing similar losses. The Society of the Compassionate Friends is for bereaved parents who need help readjusting to life after the death of a child. IMPACT (Interested Motivated Parents Against Cancer Today) is for parents of children with cancerous diseases. Alcoholics Anonymous is the group formed to encourage those struggling against alcoholism. Al-Anon is a group composed of family members learning to cope with alcoholics in their families. National SIDS (Sudden Infant Death Syndrome) Foundation, 310 South Michigan Avenue, Chicago, Illinois 60604 seeks to alleviate the guilt of parents who have lost a baby through "crib death."

There are many other groups to help divorced persons, drug abusers, and battered wives, to name a few. A word of caution: Be discerning in recommending a group to others or seeking one for yourself so that you are not lured into a religious cult.

If the church—the body of Christ—were compassionately ministering as it should, there probably would not be so many suffering people needing help today.

Importance of a Daily Walk With the Lord

Of the people who go through earthshaking experiences of grief, those whose religious faith is mature and healthy to begin with come through their grief better able to help others who face similar tragedies.

Similarly, those whose faith is immature or childish tend to face loss in an unhealthy way. Frequently they fail to work through their grief. Months, even years, later they are still fighting internal battles that the spiritually mature person has resolved.

People of mature faith do not suddenly acquire such faith when they need it. Like athletes who must stay in training, Christians must keep their faith in shape for whatever may come. When grief assails such individuals, they are ready for it.

The old Swedish hymn, "Day by Day" expresses so well how we should be facing the inevitable encounters with grief in our daily walk.

> Day by day, and with each passing moment
> Strength I find to meet my trials here;
> Trusting in my Father's wise bestowment,
> I've no cause for worry or for fear.
> He, whose heart is kind beyond all measure,
> Gives unto each day what He deems best,
> Lovingly its part of pain and pleasure,
> Mingling toil with peace and rest.

Every day the Lord Himself is near me,
With a special mercy for each hour;
All my cares He fain would bear and cheer me,
He whose name is Counsellor and Power.
The protection of His child and treasure
Is a charge that on Himself He laid;
"As thy days, thy strength shall be in measure,"
This the pledge to me He made.

Help me then, in every tribulation,
So to trust Thy promises, O Lord,
That I lose not faith's sweet consolation,
Offered me within Thy holy word.
Help me, Lord, when toil and trouble meeting,
E'er to take, as from a father's hand,
One by one, the days, the moments fleeting,
Till I reach the promised land.[22]

---

[1]*The Ann Landers Encyclopedia A to Z* (Garden City, N.Y.: Doubleday, 1978), p. 560.

[2]*Today's Health Guide,* ed. W.W. Bauer, M.D., (American Medical Association, 1965), p. 202.

[3]Franklin M. Segler, *Your Emotions and Your Faith* (Nashville, Tenn.: Broadman Press, 1970), p. 107.

[4]*Today's Health Guide,* p. 202.

[5]Segler, *Your Emotions and Your Faith,* p. 107.

[6]*Today's Health Guide,* p. 202.

[7]Colin Murray Parkes, "Death and Dying: Challenge and Change (Grief)" *The Tri-County Times* (N.J.: Times Publishing Inc., March 28, 1979).

[8]*Ibid.*

[9]*Ibid.*

[10]*Today's Health Guide,* p. 202.

[11]Frank B. Minirth, M.D. and Paul D. Meier, M.D., *Happiness Is a Choice* (Grand Rapids, Mich.: Baker, 1978), p. 37.

[12]Joni Eareckson and Steve Estes, *A Step Further* (Grand Rapids, Mich.: Zondervan, 1978), p. 97.

[13]Edith Schaeffer, *Affliction* (Old Tappan, N.J.: Revell, 1978), p. 206.

[14]*Ibid.*

[15]Joyce Landorf, *The High Cost of Growing* (Nashville, Tenn.: Thomas Nelson, 1978), p. 59.

MAKING GOOD YOUR GRIEF

[16]Philip Yancey, *Where Is God When It Hurts?* (Grand Rapids, Mich.: Zondervan, 1977), pp. 69–70.

[17]John A. Hunter, "How Should You React When the Heat's On?" *The Standard* (Sept.,1978), pp. 36–37.

[18]Eareckson and Estes, *A Step Further,* pp. 182–183.

[19]Yancey, *Where Is God When It Hurts?,* pp. 153–154.

[20]Elva McAllaster, "Helping a Friend Cope With Grief," *Moody Monthly* (May, 1977), pp. 59–63.

[21]Roy B. Zuck, "How Can I Help?" *Moody Monthly.* (February, 1977), pp. 100–102.

[22]*Songs You Love, No. 5.* (Lincoln, Neb.: Back to the Bible Publishers, 1960), pp. 8–9.

12

How Jesus Coped With Human Problems

Billy Graham once said that if he were to step on an antbed and grind a hundred ants into the dirt, he would have no way of knowing what they thought or how they felt. He has no communication with ants. He might get down on his hands and knees and peer at the anthill, but he could not know what they were saying, or if they were saying anything at all. How would they explain what had happened? How could he tell them he was sorry in a way they could understand? Because he has never been an ant, he could not answer their questions.

If it had not been for Jesus, we might conclude that God could not know anything about life here on Planet Earth—at least not in a way whereby He could feel the pain, the loneliness, and the stress that humans feel. And He certainly couldn't offer comfort to man. How could God comfort and give assurance in a compassionate, personal way if He had remained God in the heavens, never having visited the earth?

The writer to the Hebrews, in speaking of the glory of the Son of God, wrote,

But we see Jesus, who was made a little lower than the angels for the suffering of death . . . (Heb. 2:9).

Forasmuch then as the children [the writer's name for human beings] are partakers of flesh and blood, he also himself likewise took part of the same . . . (Heb. 2:14).

Wherefore in all things it behoved him to be made like unto his brethren, that he might be a merciful and faithful high priest in things pertaining to God, to make reconciliation for the sins of the people. For in that he himself hath suffered being tempted, he is able to succour them that are tempted (Heb. 2:17,18).

Several important truths are captured in these verses. First, Jesus became man, taking a position "lower than the angels," for the purpose of saving mankind. Second, He took on flesh and blood in a real body, becoming like us "in all things" for the purpose of being our "merciful and faithful" high priest. Third, He faced temptations so that He could "succour" (aid, help, befriend, support, comfort, take care of) all of us who are tempted.

This same writer later added:

Seeing then that we have a great high priest, that is passed into the heavens, Jesus the Son of God, let us hold fast our profession. For we have not an high priest which cannot be touched with the feeling of our infirmities; but was in all points tempted like as we are, yet without sin (Heb. 4: 14,15).

Note that Jesus, the Son of God, became like us *in all things* and was tempted *in all points* as we are. With confidence we can look more closely at His life as the Gospels portray Him. We can see how He responded to every test and trial that came His way. This will help us cope with life, or, as the Scripture says, "hold fast" our profession as Christians.

This chapter is the key to the studies in this book, because Jesus is our example. If He could not cope with life, then surely we cannot. But He did cope—more than that, He overcame. And we can, too, by following His example. Let us look at the ways He confronted the dilemmas of living.

Verbal Confrontation

The Scriptures are silent about the first thirty years of the life of Jesus, except for one incident in his twelfth year. Luke tells us (chapter two) that He accompanied His parents on the annual pilgrimage to Jerusalem and that when they and other family members left to return home, He remained in Jerusalem. They did not miss Him until their second day on the road, supposing that He was with other relatives in the caravan. When a search for Him revealed no clues, they retraced their steps to the temple where, on the following day, they found Him. He was "sitting in the midst of the doctors [teachers of the Law], both hearing them, and asking them questions" (Luke 2:46). The Scriptures says "all that heard him were astonished at his understanding and answers" (Luke 2:47). Mary and Joseph were astonished, too, and not a little annoyed.

Their confrontation did not affect Him any more than did the profound learning of the teachers of Israel. The Scripture says that it was Mary who addressed him, saying, "Son, why hast thou thus dealt with us? behold, thy father and I have sought thee sorrowing" (Luke 2:48).

His answer is classic—simple, unapologetic, not in the least disrespectful, but fully showing that He knew who He was and what He was about. "How is it that ye sought me?" he responded. "Wist ye not that I must be about my Father's business?" (Luke 2:49). In His answer we can see the purposefulness of the Son of God, as He began to assume the role for which He had come to earth. Mary and Joseph had been warned by angelic beings at His birth of the nature of this Son of theirs. Jesus was merely going about His Father's business.

Other places in the Gospels show that Jesus was always master of the situation. When He dealt with the crafty Pharisees and scribes, He never fell into their traps, nor did

He sin by slandering them. Before Pilate, He maintained strength. In every verbal confrontation, He was in control. He did this by leaning on His heavenly Father for wisdom. That kind of wisdom and help has not been withdrawn; it is ours for the asking.

"If any of you lack wisdom, let him ask of God, that giveth to all men liberally, and upbraideth not; and it shall be given him" (James 1:5).

Family Pressures

Eighteen years after the events in Jerusalem, a wedding took place in Cana of Galilee. The apostle John recorded what happened on this occasion of Jesus' first miracle, the transformation of tepid Galilean water into wine.

The few details that are given in John 2 tell us that a wedding took place and that Jesus, His mother, and His disciples were invited. These occasions were festive and usually lasted several days. It was a time of laughter and feasting. But the wine did not last! In order to save the host from embarrassment, Mary apparently pushed Jesus to perform a miracle. The Bible says she told Him, evidently in the presence of the house servants, that the wine had run out. Then she addressed the servants: ". . . Whatsoever he saith unto you, do it" (John 2:5).

Was Mary acting upon her knowledge of who He was? Jesus told her his "hour" was not yet come. Remaining calm, He conveyed to her that He knew when and how to reveal Himself to Israel and that He needed no help from her, even if she were His mother. Having said that, He proceeded to do what she may have hoped He would do. He turned the water to wine.

By intervening, Mary reveals her motherly instinct. Jesus let her know that He was a man and that He would not be pushed. Other episodes show even more clearly how He

162

withstood the pressures of family. Once, at the height of Jesus' popularity (Mark 3:31–35), His mother and some of His brothers appeared at the fringes of a huge crowd and tried to call Him outside to them. Many Bible students infer that Jesus' family was embarrassed to have Him making such a spectacle of Himself (the crowds had been saying Jesus might be demon-possessed); they wanted to take Him home and end all the rumors. But He did not submit to their demands, nor did He speak ill of them. Upon learning of their presence, He said, ". . . Who is my mother, or my brethren? . . . Whosoever shall do the will of God, the same is my brother, and my sister, and mother." He continued teaching and healing the sick.

John records that, as opposition to Jesus grew, especially in the city of Jerusalem and its surrounding area, Jesus chose to remain in comparative obscurity in Galilee. A feast was approaching, and his brothers tried reasoning with Him. They told Him, as if He had never thought of it, that if He wanted to make Himself known He ought to go to Jerusalem and there work some of His miracles (John 7:1–9). They were putting pressure on Him, but He ignored their counsel.

A Christian can face intense pressure from family members when he begins to follow Jesus. While family members usually mean well, they may simply not understand, especially if they are not believers. Jesus would counsel you to remain respectful to your parents; so long as you are under their authority, you should obey them. But He talks often enough about self-denial and the cost of discipleship to make clear that we must not allow family pressures to keep us from doing what He says.

Social Embarrassment

The wedding at Cana offers insights into how Jesus coped with a potentially embarrassing situation—the lack of wine at a Middle Eastern wedding feast.

As mentioned earlier, it seems Mary was trying to push the Lord into this miracle. We can assume that He intended to work this "sign" anyway, and it is to His credit that He did the thing His mother recommended. The act shows that He did not want anyone to be embarrassed in the situation—neither the host who depended upon the supply of wine for the happiness of his guests, nor His mother who apparently said what she did in the presence of a number of other people. We can see that Jesus was concerned for individuals. That kind of loving concern on our parts will enable us to cope with ticklish social situations. Concern for others is always in superb taste.

Physical Appetites

The Bible is careful to give us a well-rounded assessment of Jesus. One thing is clear, Jesus was fully a man, with the capacity to become hungry (Matt. 4:2; Mark 11:12), to become tired (John 4:6), to weep (John 11:35), to need sleep (Matt. 8:24), and to enjoy the companionship of others. Following His baptism by John, Jesus was led by the Spirit into the desert. There He was tempted by the devil after going without food forty days and nights. In Matthew 4 and Luke 4 we see Satan approach Jesus with three temptations. First, he tempted the Lord to satisfy His normal physical appetite. ". . .If thou be the Son of God, command that these stones be made bread" (Matt. 4:3).

Jesus, knowing that He was being tempted, responded: ". . . It is written, Man shall not live by bread alone, but by every word that proceedeth out of the mouth of God" (Matt. 4:4).

What an example to us who are tempted every day to follow our physical appetites. Our bodies are good, and our appetites are given to us by the Creator; but we all need self-control so that we do not become slaves to our physical appetites. As a man, Jesus must have had the capacity to be attracted to women, but lust is never even suggested in all of His relationships with females. He held His bodily appetites in check, so that He could fulfill His life purpose. He never gave in to gluttony or to procrastination or to laziness. If there was a temptation within the physical realm that He might have been more susceptible to than to any other, surely it was the temptation to drive Himself too hard. He had a world to save, and He had only thirty-three years to do it. But there was no panic in His pace. He even chose to take the disciples away on occasion for a rest, because the people would not leave Him alone (Mark 6:31).

Jesus would counsel us to discipline our physical appetites and live a balanced life. The Word of God is the guide for our actions and is our best weapon against the enemy.

Pride

In the wilderness, the devil came back a second time and tempted Jesus to show off His miraculous power. In Matthew 4:6 he said, ". . .If thou be the Son of God, cast thyself down: for it is written, He shall give his angels charge concerning thee . . ." (Matt. 4:6).

Satan quoted a Psalm, but he quoted in error, omitting the key phrase "to keep thee in all thy ways" (Ps. 91:11). Jesus was not fooled. He could see that to do such a thing would only cater to man's obsession for the sensational and would do little to win committed, lifelong disciples. He resisted this temptation again by saying, ". . . It is written again, Thou shalt not tempt the Lord thy God" (Matt. 4:7).

No one is exempt from Satan's subtle and persistent suggestion that we indulge our pride. From every side today man is being told: "You deserve it; take care of Number One." If we cultivate a close relationship to Jesus, we will be able to detect the snares the devil lays for us, and we will be able to cope with temptations of pride.

False Worship

In the wilderness experience, there was the temptation to worship something other than God. For Jesus, the temptation was to bow the knee to Satan. The reward for so doing seemed great; after all, Jesus had come to save the world and its kingdoms and here Satan was offering Him all of the world *without the suffering of the cross!* But Jesus saw through this deception and again reminded Satan, ". . . it is written, Thou shalt worship the Lord thy God, and him only shalt thou serve" (Matt. 4:10).

Israel's seventy years in Babylon cured her of idolatry. Following her return to Palestine in the fifth century B.C., she was never again accused of idol worship. Satan, seeing he could not corrupt the Jews with idols of wood and stone, sought more subtle means.

Anything that comes between man and God is an idol, an object of false worship. We have seen that Jesus would not bow to Satan's tactics, nor would he give in to the pressures of his family. He resisted the temptation of giving allegiance to anything but His Father.

Western man is not much tempted to bow down before stone idols. He worships instead his own intellect, his body, himself. The tenets of his faith are the high-sounding phrases of humanism, which teach him to trust his own "enlightened" reasoning rather than God and to make decisions according to "situational ethics" rather than on the basis of the absolute Word of God. Such humanism is no less pagan than idolatry.

Jesus always guided men toward worship of the Father, whether in conversation with the Samaritan woman (John 4) or with His disciples (John 15,16). Paul warned the first-century Christians that the world of men "worshipped and served the creature more than the Creator . . ." (Rom. 1:25). Jesus' words give us the greatest assurance of victory over false systems of worship, for He counsels us: ". . . seek ye first the kingdom of God, and His righteousness . . ." (Matt. 6:33).

Rejection

No one will be called upon to handle rejection as unremitting as Jesus encountered. At one point in His life He was considered by the religious establishment to be *guilty until proven innocent*. ". . . The world was made by him, and the world knew him not. He came unto his own, and his own received him not" (John 1:10,11).

How did He cope with such rejection?

At the outset of His ministry He appeared in His home town of Nazareth to read the Scriptures. The text for that day was from Isaiah 61 and was clearly prophetic. It said, in part, that the Messiah would come, and that He would "preach the gospel to the poor . . . heal the brokenhearted . . . preach deliverance to the captives, and recovering of sight to the blind . . . set at liberty them that are bruised . . . [and] preach the acceptable year of the Lord" (Luke 4:18,19). After concluding the reading, Jesus said, "This day is this scripture fulfilled in your ears" (Luke 4:21).

How did the townsfolk welcome these words? Did they open their hearts to Him? No, quite the opposite. They were offended by Him. "Is not this Joseph's son?" (Luke 4:22) they asked, as they tried to take Him by force and throw Him off a cliff. Scripture does not indicate that He ever returned to Nazareth.

He faced intense opposition from the leaders within Jewish religion, but He was not intimidated by their threats. Although it was dangerous for Him to appear in the Jerusalem area, He nevertheless went there (John 7; John 12). He answered accusations in His public discourses and debates so ably that there came a time when the scribes and Pharisees dared not ask Him any more questions (Luke 20:40). He coped with their rejection by engaging them in debate and winning every argument, as well as by walking courageously throughout the countryside on His Father's business.

Jesus coped with rejection in other ways. His own disciple, Judas, betrayed Him, but Jesus showed more hurt than He did vindictiveness. His close apostle, Peter, denied Him, but Jesus grieved for him and later sought him out and restored him to service. All the disciples left Him, but He prayed for them. When He was accused by the religionists, including the high priest, and by Pilate, He remained silent. Isaiah prophesied this of the suffering Servant: "He was oppressed, and he was afflicted, yet he opened not his mouth: he is brought as a lamb to the slaughter, and as a sheep before her shearers is dumb, so he openeth not his mouth" (Isa. 53:7).

We do well to think of Jesus' example so that we will not be intimidated or discouraged when we are rejected by others. The best defense is to keep our mouths shut and our prayer lives active.

Rights

This is the age of rights—civil rights, women's rights, gay rights, teacher's rights. The prevailing attitude is, if you get a "raw deal" in marriage, you have the right to a divorce. If you get a "raw deal" at work, you have the right to strike.

Jesus had rights, too. As the Son of God, he had the right to reign over the entire world. "A ruin, ruin, ruin I will make it; there shall not be even a trace of it until he comes whose right it is; and to him I will give it" (Ezek. 21:27 RSV).

As a human, He had the right to privacy, a home, friends, protection of the law, respect, and credibility. But He willingly relinquished His rights to everything and disciplined Himself for the task for which He came. If we would be His disciples, dare we stand up for our rights?

For one is approved if, mindful of God, he endures pain while suffering unjustly. For what credit is it, if when you do wrong and are beaten for it you take it patiently? But if when you do right and suffer for it you take it patiently, you have God's approval. For to this you have been called, because Christ also suffered for you, leaving you an example, that you should follow in his steps. He committed no sin; no guile was found on his lips. When he was reviled, he did not revile in return; when he suffered, he did not threaten; but he trusted to him who judges justly. He himself bore our sins in his body on the tree, that we might die to sin and live to righteousness (1 Pet. 2:19–24).

Insecurity

Jesus chose the insecure status of an itinerant rabbi. Only He can know what a great contrast His life on earth was to that close fellowship He had had with the Father before His incarnation. At best, we can only speculate. At one point, Jesus told a scribe who would follow Him: "The foxes have holes, and the birds of the air have nests; but the Son of man hath not where to lay his head" (Matt. 8:20). When He left Nazareth, He no longer had a place that He could call His own. But He exuded confidence, poise, and stability, for He knew who He was and where He was going.

The song writer, L. M. Hollingsworth, has captured this truth in the hymn "The Cross Was His Own."

> They borrowed a bed to lay His Head
> when Christ the Lord came down;
> They borrowed the ass in the mountain pass
> for Him to ride to town.
> He borrowed the bread when the crowd He fed
> on the grassy mountainside;
> He borrowed the dish of broken fish
> with which He satisfied.
> He borrowed the ship in which to sit
> to teach the multitude;

He borrowed a nest in which to rest
    He had never a home so rude.
He borrowed a room on His way to the tomb
    the Passover Lamb to eat;
They borrowed a cave for Him a grave,
    they borrowed a winding sheet.
But the crown that He wore and the cross that He bore
    were His own.[1]

We are called pilgrims and strangers in the earth (1 Pet. 2:11). As such, we experience insecurity, but we know that Jesus experienced it in far greater measure than we. This will encourage us to keep our minds firmly fixed upon Him.

The Storms of Life

In a day when the people were superstitious about such unpredictable elements as the weather, Jesus showed no fear. The most outstanding example of this is the incident on the Sea of Galilee when Jesus fell asleep in the boat with His disciples (Matt. 8:23–27; Mark 4:35–41; Luke 8:22–25). A raging storm swept down upon them, and the men, many of them seasoned fishermen, feared for their lives. Luke says they awoke Jesus and cried, ". . . Master, master, we perish . . ." (Luke 8:24). That Jesus could sleep while the boat was tossing in the raging sea and the stormy winds were howling, indicates His perfect love relationship with His Father. ". . . Perfect love casteth out fear . . ." (1 John 4:18). Completely free of fear and panic, He motioned to the wind and the waves, "and there was a great calm" (Matt. 8:26). The effect of Jesus' power over the elements was so great that the disciples were afraid. They said, ". . . What manner of man is this! for he commandeth even the winds and the water, and they obey him" (Luke 8:25).

Jesus knew how to cope with cosmic fury: The power He

170

demonstrated at sea can carry over into the everyday storms of our lives. Jesus coped by resting in the Father. Later, prior to His betrayal and trial, a storm of a different nature brewed about Him; but He walked into the charged atmosphere of Jerusalem at the time of the Feast of the Passover, still teaching, still doing good, still showing loving concern for the individual. Frequently throughout the gospel accounts, we are told that Jesus went aside to pray. I have no doubt that His steady, unbroken fellowship with the Father gave Him poise and strength to remain calm and in command in the midst of stormy controversy.

In June, 1978, the well-known pastor and television preacher Robert Schuller was in Korea with his wife, ministering to Korean pastors. Their tour was cut short when they learned that halfway across the world one of their five children, thirteen-year-old Carol, had been in a motorcycle accident and that the doctors had had to amputate the girl's lower left leg. The Schullers have told how they were comforted by the prayers of the Korean Christians and by the Scripture passage that one pastor gave them as they boarded a plane for the United States. The text was the familiar Romans 8:28, "And we know that all things work together for good to them that love God, to them who are the called according to his purpose."

The strain and agony of this devoted mother and father would have been too great, they say, but for the comfort of the Holy Spirit during that trying hour. Most of all, they hurt for their little girl and feared that she would be overcome emotionally by having to undergo surgery without her mom and dad to comfort her. Within two days they were at Carol's bedside. In the book *The Courage of Carol,* they tell how their daughter's radiant courage and faith inspired them during the ordeal. Reverend Schuller speaks of the strength his daughter had drawn from the many Scripture verses she had committed to memory in the church's Bible school and through home Bible readings; he says these promises kept his daughter from severe doubt and depression.

This kind of inner strength against the storms of life is what we can build through Christ. Even when facing storms of cosmic fury, we need not fear; we can command the winds and the elements to do us no harm in the name of Jesus Christ. Jesus set the pattern, and we can follow.

Pain

Jesus knew how to handle pain. This ought to be a great comfort to those who have much pain in their lives. The accounts of the Crucifixion in all four Gospels indicate that Jesus was whipped (scourged) with a Roman cat-o'-nine-tails, slapped, and spit upon. He was ridiculed by the rough soldiers, and one of them crushed a crown of thorns down upon His innocent head. Having gone without sleep and food since the Last Supper, He was weak when He was given the heavy cross to drag up Calvary's hill. He fell beneath its weight. At the top of the hill, He was stretched out upon that rough cross. Soldiers took His hands—tough hands that knew the hard labor of woodworking, tender hands that had touched the blind and the ill and made them well—and laid them palm up upon the wood, driving heavy spikes through them into the wood. His feet were likewise nailed to that cruel cross, which was then uprighted and allowed to sink into the hole which had been dug for it. The pain must have been excruciating.

Under the scorching Judean sun He hung upon the cross. Isaiah, in prophesying of Him, said, ". . . many were astonished at him—his appearance was so marred, beyond human semblance, and his form beyond that of the sons of men" (Isa. 52:14 RSV). Pain shot through every nerve and muscle of His body. Those who were crucified usually died of suffocation. As one's body weakened, it would sag until

172

eventually the victim could no longer breathe. To permit air to enter His lungs, Jesus had to press down upon the nails in His feet and push His body up, which caused maddening pain. This He endured, because He loved us. Without screaming or moaning, He suffered it all. He did not want man's sympathy. Even as He endured this torture, He cried out, ". . . Father, forgive them; for they know not what they do" (Luke 23:34).

John, in writing of these things, recalls that Jesus said, ". . . shall I not drink the cup which the Father has given me?" (John 18:11, rsv). No, He would not refuse the humiliation and the pain. How else would He be able to identify with us in the burdens that weigh us down, the shadows that darken our paths, the hurt that threatens to strangle the heart!

An unknown poet has written:

> Out of the presses of pain,
>   Cometh the soul's best wine;
> And the eyes that have shed no rain,
>   Can shed but little shine.

Hate

One of the severest tests that any person can endure is the hatred of others. Jesus endured this. Even though everything He did should have caused people to love Him, certain ones hated Him enough to plot His murder and carry out the illegal execution. Early in His ministry He warned His followers, "Woe unto you, when all men shall speak well of you! for so did their fathers to the false prophets" (Luke 6:26). In the next verses He offered the key to coping with hatred. It is the simple rule:

. . . Love your enemies, do good to them which hate you, Bless them that curse you, and pray for them which despitefully use

173

you. . . . But love ye your enemies, and do good, and lend, hoping for nothing again; and your reward shall be great, and ye shall be the children of the Highest: for he is kind unto the unthankful and *to* the evil. Be ye therefore merciful, as your Father also is merciful (Luke 6:27,28,35,36).

To be the object of another's scorn is painful indeed. To be at the other end of someone's pointing finger is unpleasant, and to bear hurtful things without retaliation requires determined effort.

There are helpful words in the Old Testament Book of Nahum: ". . .The Lord hath his way in the whirlwind and in the storm. . ." (Nah. 1:3). He can be trusted to take care of our enemies, those who hate us without cause. "The Lord is good, a stronghold in the day of trouble; and he knoweth them that trust in him" (Nah. 1:7).

Jesus always exhibited an unwavering confidence in the Father. Our God is a God of boundless resources; the only limits are imposed by us. Our expectations are too limited, and our praying too little. Not so with Jesus, as He turned His face upward to seek God's help. Jesus moved on in spite of opposition. At one point He instructed the disciples to literally "shake off the dust under your feet for a testimony against them" (Mark 6:11) when they encountered those who would not hear them nor respond kindly.

"Don't waste your time nor your emotional resources," He was telling the disciples. How much emotional strain we needlessly endure as we try to cope with those whose treatment leaves much to be desired. Far better to follow Jesus' example.

This is not to say that Jesus was trying to run away from His problems. To the contrary, Jesus on other occasions spoke up fearlessly against His opponents and called them "hyprocrites" (Mark 7:6).

The hallmark of Jesus' life was His abundant capacity to

love the unloving. In answer to the scribe who asked which was the greatest commandment, Jesus answered with these familiar words: ". . . Thou shalt love thy neighbor as thyself . . ." (Mark 12:31). Love for the Lord, first of all, and then love for others—this is the answer to coping with hatred.

Loneliness

Finally, Jesus understood loneliness.

The Scripture tells us that many nights He went out alone to pray. He was more alone than any man, for even those closest to Him did not understand Him. He was a solitary figure.

Jesus' loneliness came to a climax on the cross when even His heavenly Father turned from Him as He became the sin-bearer. In this moment of anguish Jesus cried, ". . . My God, my God, why hast thou forsaken me?" (Mark 15:34). In becoming sin for us (2 Cor. 5:21), He bore the rejection of His own Father, something none of us will ever have to bear unless we reject Jesus. This was His lonely walk through "the valley of the shadow of death." But even then He feared no evil, for He trusted in the Father's faithfulness and power to effect His resurrection and eternal glory.

Jesus knew how to cope with loneliness, and you can also. In fact, He has firsthand knowledge of every problem we have. Jesus can say, "I walked that path before you. I had that feeling before. That sorrow is great, and I know all about it. I know your pain, your tension, your loneliness, your temptation not to believe. I know what you are doing and what you are going through; I love you and will see you through."

---

[1]*Songs You Love, No. 3*, comp. Eugene L. Clark (Lincoln, Neb.: Back to the Bible Publishers, 1958), p. 30. Used by permission.